A Social Onto-Epistemology

STUDIES ON CULTURE TECHNOLOGY AND EDUCATION

Edited by Krzysztof Abriszewski

VOLUME 9

PETER LANG

Mariola Kuszyk-Bytniewska

A Social Onto-Epistemology

Translated by Maciej Smoczyński

PETER LANG

Bibliographic Information published by the Deutsche Nationalbibliothek
The Deutsche Nationalbibliothek lists this publication in the Deutsche
Nationalbibliografie; detailed bibliographic data is available in the internet
at http://dnb.d-nb.de.

Library of Congress Cataloging-in-Publication Data
A CIP catalog record for this book has been applied for at the
Library of Congress.

This publication was financially supported by Maria Curie-Skłodowska University.

The cover image courtesy of Benjamin ben Chaim.

ISSN 2196-5129
ISBN 978-3-631-88698-4 (Print)
E-ISBN 978-3-631-89999-1 (E-PDF)
E-ISBN 978-3-631-90000-0 (EPUB)
DOI 10.3726/b20898

© Peter Lang GmbH
Internationaler Verlag der Wissenschaften
Berlin 2023
All rights reserved.

Peter Lang – Berlin · Lausannae · Bruxelles · New York · Oxford · Warszawa

This publication has been peer reviewed.

www.peterlang.com

Contents

Preface

This book has an interdisciplinary character. It concerns the border area between philosophy and social sciences, among which sociology occupies a prominent place.

Social onto-epistemology is a polemical answer to classical, traditional divisions within philosophy, which, as the history of philosophy shows, separate ontology from epistemology, alternately giving priority to one or the other. Classical philosophy, rooted in the intellectual impulse of antiquity, gave priority to ontology, while early modern philosophy privileged the theory of cognition. Following the rise of empirical sciences on the human being in the 19th century, sociology, along with other social sciences, got squeezed into the Cartesian paradigm perpetuating the primacy of epistemology as the first philosophy. Even well into the 20th century, the primacy of epistemology was understood quite traditionally: as a privilege of specific, philosophical insight into sciences allowing for their validation. The price to pay for it turned out in the form of "epistemocentrism" and "scholastic ethnocentrism". This is how Pierre Bourdieu called an approach privileging constrained, scholarly (i.e. created in the scholars' community) point of view, which dismisses all kinds of reconstructions of practical approach to knowledge, exercised by people investigated by scholars. In "Pascalian Meditations" Bourdieu consciously referred not only to Pascal, but also to Cartesian tradition (Descartes and Husserl). Scholastic, in Bourdieu's terms, point of view, itself meditatively detached from social life, establishes norms of description. These norms re-evaluate the scholar's point of view, carrying the intellectual burden of his/her experiences and research practices, and on the other hand, they re-evaluate the priority of epistemology as an area of validating scientific knowledge, an area where standards of scientific knowledge are forged. This state of affairs only perpetuates a certain form of a contradiction within scientific cognition: it is ready to reconstruct practical knowledge, but only by means of scholastic knowledge, inadequate to the subject matter. The theoretical value of Bourdieu's attacks depends on the fact that he questions the very core of epistemocentric tradition, using resources provided by social sciences. Thus epistemocentrism and scholasticism in theories describing social reality become a trap. To use Gaston Bachelard's terms, it is an "epistemological obstacle" and the source of recurring crises of social theories' self-awareness.

In my understanding, the cardinal sin of epistemocentrism is overlooking ontic properties of objects investigated by social sciences, namely, that they are social tissue woven by different subjects' actions. Social actors' knowledge motivates their actions, but also inevitably takes part in constituting them as subjects.

Onto-epistemological transgression of epistemocentrism in the area of sociology, as I see it, is reaching beyond it for manners of conceptualising social life in categories of objectivity, rationality and intersubjectivity, as both ontological and epistemological qualifications. In my project it entails modifying meanings of these notions to encompass relations between manners of being and constituting subjects with modalities of knowledge and self-knowledge, which the modern and post-modern forms of common, social life environment make foundations of contemporary subjectivity forms. Sociology is a special science, because it produces sure knowledge about its theoretically constituted objects, and, at the same time, it reciprocally changes that knowledge which serves practical constitution of subjects participating in social realities. In other words, sociology is a sort of knowledge that produces certain knowledge of social reality, which, circulating in society, reflexively changes sociology. Sociology, then, in its meta-reflection, reaches for philosophy and thereby lies a problem: a discrepancy between research practice and reflection on it. Philosophical thought on sociology considers knowledge that it provides and strives to place it in a general, broader order of knowledge. But knowledge so severed from the conditions of its production and described in a quasi-objectivist way (modelled on natural sciences) stops making sense. Therefore, since the emergence of the discipline, sociology struggled with its status as knowledge; epistemocentrically oriented philosophical thought on science could not grasp that specificity. Early modern philosophy was not able to recognise the communitarian dimension of sociological and social study, whereas the individualist, Cartesian epistemology was blind to that background.

Shortly, philosophical reflection on social study was one-sided, hence newly born sciences of man (the 19th century), validated with tools of early modern philosophy, were bound for failure. To explain the status and describe the identity of social sciences, not only cognitive involvement of theory is necessary, but also ontic. Hence epistemology and ontology need to be combined in meta-reflection on knowledge about society. On the other hand, social reality is an indispensable component of social study. Nowadays, the concept of creating knowledge independent from human (cultural, social) environment has been largely abandoned, and rightly so. Nobody today believes in pure science, uninvolved, distanced from values and meanings, whether on the side of the subject or the object, thus, from the human world, from culture, even in so-called hard sciences. Hence my proposition is to extend and enrich the notion of cognition, to notice and take into account its part in creating social reality. This proposition is what I call social onto-epistemology. Social onto-epistemology is the unity of ontic determination of social study and epistemic determination of social being. Who is the one who investigates and what/who is investigated? The answer to these questions, inevitable in social life, always influences the process of forging the social world, it shapes social reality.

The critique of the Cartesian idea of subjectivity, the critique of the epistemological relation founding the monadic *Cogito*'s being, which assumed the form of controversy between traditional philosophy of science and sociology of science and sociology of knowledge (so-called *science wars*) are this book's recurring themes. In early modernity, the close ties of social, ethical and political practice with the development of knowledge were deemed an obstacle in perfecting science. The care for method led to the separation of theoretical and practical tasks of science, and to the conclusion that knowledge is a result of the marriage between *episteme* and *techne*. This engendered universalism based on the Cartesian belief in one world and one science describing it, a science stemming from the trunk of metaphysics, but gradually eliminated from its area. Kant's criticism basically closes this process. It caused effects that neither Descartes nor Kant could think of. These results included abandoning the ontic foundation of science, filling the blanks in social sciences with prosthetic naturalistic models, seeking makeshift technologies and their social applications, instrumental understanding of technology and experience.

This was supported by strong philosophical need for systemic ordering of knowledge, accompanying the process of sciences' differentiation and their divorces with philosophy. As epistemology was granted primacy to other areas of philosophy and cognition was granted primacy to other areas of subject-shaping human activity, action finally became separated from investigation wherever action was construed as *techne*, as opposed to *praxis*.

Therefore, in this book I perform a kind of re-evaluation of social sciences' self-awareness, leaning above all on Pierre Bourdieu's and Florian Znaniecki's concepts, but indirectly also on Norbert Elias, Anthony Giddens and Charles Taylor, along with Stanisław Ossowski, Marek Siemek and Barbara Tuchańska. Analysing models of knowledge, Aristotle's and Descartes's, I try to portray how the privileged position of cognition theory in European philosophy was acquired, and what it means for social and ethical knowledge, as well as how ontic moments of cognition became marginalised within this knowledge.

Ancient and early modern sciences grew on the same, however historically differentiated, ground, which is human life environment. Whereas Aristotle's pluralistic model of knowledge allowed scientific grasp of "things capable of being otherwise", Descartes's unitary model didn't anymore. Within post-Cartesian philosophy this common ground was a priori eliminated as a potential epistemological obstacle invalidating the strategy of philosophical criticism. Knowledge and investigation are thus separated from action, science should be uninvolved, distanced, cleansed of what concerns *praxis*. In early modernity, *poiesis* was reduced to *techne*, and scientific knowledge identified with *episteme* supported with *techne*, while *praxis* was refused a place among sciences.

In the further part of the book, I show the transformation of social thought, whereby basic categories describing social reality (rationality, intersubjectivity, objectivity), morph from epistemological into ontoepistemological concepts. Nevertheless, in the area of social sciences, especially in sociology, a new kind of discourse is still missing, ontoepistemological discourse. Only through such a discourse intersubjectivity can reveal its bond with rationality and objectivity in a way that does not produce obstacles and paradoxes in sociologists' thinking. Instead of overt or tacit use of the *ego cogito* figure, it is worthwhile to realise the ontically limited character of human rationality. Then we can reveal ethicality (widely understood, in the sense of Greek *ethos*), which is an indispensable component of intersubjectivity. In this new perspective, we should also describe objectivity as a historical, contingent category of our cognitions and forms of knowledge, a category entangled in changes affecting forms of subjectivity (being a subject). Finally, in onto-epistemological discourse we can describe the basic sense of rationality, hinting that it grasps not only cognitive aspects of subjective reference, but also ontic, existential forms of self-reference.

What is interesting for me is that very co-dependence: creating new, onto-epistemological perspective of social research under the influence of new phenomena in the domain of social realities, which are in turn the object of that research. Just as 19th-century social processes forged sociology seeking a rightful place among other scientific disciplines, the social processes that we are taking part in today, are, in my view, the base for reorientation of social sciences. I agree with Florian Znaniecki (whom I consider a precursor of onto-epistemological research), when he states that social reality always exists as someone's reality, that is, examining its social aspect we must involve the humanistic coefficient, the fact of (co-)being, (co-)investigation and (co-)action. One cannot produce a reasonable social theory overlooking the fact that social reality is (co-)created and (co-) maintained by social actors, who are not only investigating agents, but above all acting subjects, ontically located in communities, cultures, languages, *grosso modo* in co-constituting practices.

Rationality, intersubjectivity and objectivity are, as I aim to prove, basic onto-epistemological categories, expressing anew the specific link between a social theory and its object. Transgressing such old dualisms as subject – object, structure – agency, representationism – constructivism, naturalism – idealism (anti-realism), investigation – action, macrosociology – microsociology, the Platonian "separation" (*chorismos*) and "participation" (*methexis*), I strive to determine onto-epistemological entry conditions of sociological thought. Rationality, intersubjectivity and objectivity are categories that characterise both intelligible properties of social being as an object of investigation, and ontic properties of investigating agents, including scientific study.

Social onto-epistemology is the subject matter of my habilitation thesis from 2015, published by Wydawnictwo UMCS (Marie Curie University

Press) in Lublin, Poland. The presented work is an abridged version of the dissertation, it constitutes the quintessence of the project which I call social onto-epistemology. Nevertheless, some of its chapters were extended, others rewritten, other still removed. However, I hope the presented book forms a consequent whole embracing and describing my concept (project) of social onto-epistemology.

Chapter I A Glimpse Backwards – Onto-Epistemological Threads in Social Philosophy

Onto-epistemology is not an entirely new intellectual project, with history not reaching beyond the realm of modernity. On the contrary, ideas that may be seen as resources of onto-epistemology, can be found as early as in the antiquity, as well as in modern philosophical thought, dominated to a high degree by epistemological purists. This introductory observation must, however, be annotated with a restriction: although in the past onto-epistemological conceptualisations of reality used to be formulated, most often they were not developed or honed and for various historic reasons they did not form an easy-to-spot field of problems, a discipline or an intellectual tradition with a distinct image. Their history is rather one of marginal thoughts and abandoned concepts, and on the other hand, a history of cognitive obstacles and residues of adopted concepts situated among more important and better-articulated problems of those, still pre-modern, eras. The historical borderline, beyond which the onto-epistemological issues could no longer be ignored, was marked by the intellectual revolt of modernity. Thanks to it, cultural roles of knowledge were discovered and, in general, the meaning of knowledge reaching beyond purely cognitive functions. The onto-epistemological conceptualisation of social reality enters the area of social sciences following the discovery of consequences caused by knowledge metamorphoses and metamorphoses of its functions in the modern social world. Nevertheless, certain threads of onto-epistemology have persisted in Western intellectual culture. Before unripe and ignored, they reveal their creative potential only in the modern world of thought. Therefore each historical reconstruction in this area is prone to anachronical deformations, reconstructions of missing fragments that possibly quench the contemporary inquisitiveness, but at the same time, they confirm the thin link between onto-epistemological thought and the past.

In the historical perspective, it is interesting to find the reasons for neglect and the sources of immaturity of the onto-epistemological conceptualisation of knowledge, one that by inertia accumulated in the interpretational resources of social agents, but without its distinct theoretical articulation. Thus a question arises about the reasons for reluctance to theoretically continue those of its threads that had already acquired their articulated form. Equally interesting is the persistence of such issues in Western thought, even when they dwell on the outskirts of its main areas. It is not only about social practice and those forms which did not impose the subject of relations between cognition and being in their social form. It is also about historic shapes of knowledge, about the archaic (ancient and later, but still pre-modern) model of studying social reality. "Something" has happened in modernity, in knowledge itself and in social life, if the onto-epistemological problems have begun to pace towards the centre of contemporary understanding of social sciences.

I am going to answer the question about the past of that "something" by presenting two seemingly the most articulate and the most influential models of knowledge in Western philosophy, ones that address social sciences in their own specific ways: Aristotelian and Cartesian models. They involve the point of view of onto-epistemology, and yet they block its theoretical form. I call the first, conceived by Aristotle, a pluralistic model of knowledge, and the second, devised by Descartes, a unitary model. The intention of the former is to depict diverse forms of relations between life and knowledge (*bios praktikos* – *bios theoretikos*). The latter, in turn, shows the existence of the subject of knowledge in a way that does not allow identifying the epistemic moment in the life of the subject of knowledge, because this life as a whole becomes an act of thought: to be meant to be a subject of acts of thought or knowledge. Both models contain a certain element that can be called an ontic moment of its theoretical motivation. My purpose is to expose that moment and to attempt to describe the context of its unfulfilled historic destiny.

These introductory notes must be completed by another restriction: the influence of the mentioned models on theoretical knowledge about social life, although indirect and often hardly expressed, was constant, and thus meaningful. For many centuries they have shaped something that, to paraphrase C.W. Mills,[1] could be called social sciences' epistemological

---

1   Cf. Charles Wright Mills, *The Sociological Imagination* (40th anniversary ed.),

imagination. However these models have functioned differently in relation to knowledge about the society, each within the framework of its own tradition, they have shaped this imagination, describing the points of departure, directions of reasoning, the borders of social sciences' discourses and their purposes other than building knowledge.

1. The pluralistic model of knowledge and its ontic-ontological motivation: Aristotle

Aristotle's model of knowledge (concerning not only social life, but also knowledge as a whole) can be called pluralistic for that basic reason that it portrays knowledge as irreducibly diverse: heterogeneous in the ways it refers to its subject matters, as well as adopting different forms depending on the purposes it may serve in various areas of non-scientific human activity. This model, never explicitly expressed, harbours views on knowledge reflecting the ontic diversity of social reality and the empirical multiplicity of actual political systems, forms of ethos, convictions of the meaning of political knowledge, as well as the wide array of its conceptualisations by contemporaneous social actors. Epistemological pluralism was, thus, a consequence of Aristotle's belief in the ontic diversity of entities and the necessary diversification of ways to understand them, but, more than anything, it stemmed from the conviction of a human being's different cognitive abilities in reference to different kinds of entities. The image is completed by a certain historically and culturally limited motivation: something that perhaps without exaggeration can be called political narrow-mindedness of Greek political thought. That thought, conceiving multiple models of life within the Greek *koine*, at the same time (almost) neglected the whole non-Greek world, the barbaric world, by default attributing only negative characteristics to it.

Motivated this way, Aristotle's thought distinguishes three basic kinds of knowledge known to the Greeks[2]: theoretical, practical and productive.

Oxford University Press, Oxford 2000.

2 The division of knowledge into theoretical, practical and productive is elaborated by Aristotle in *The Nicomachean Ethics* [book VI], in *Topics* [145 a 15, 157 a 10], in *Metaphysics* [1064 a 10, 1025 b 21 and n., 1026 b 5, 1064 a 17]. Cf. Aristotle, *The Nicomachean Ethics*, trans. David Ross, Revised

In doing so he takes into account the main human abilities and duties, that is: observation or contemplation of reality (*theoria*), activity (*praxis*) and production (*poiesis*). Within the domain of what may be an object of knowledge, he distinguished two basic types: general and necessary (those "incapable of being otherwise") and non-necessary (those which "capable of being otherwise"). He intends to include the latter in his considerations, as well as the former, and he situates them in the areas of practical and productive sciences. Moreover, Aristotle imposes another distinction on these divisions, referring to two modes of life: *bios praktikos* and *bios theoretikos*. It is in them that knowledge reveals its completely different roles in life: it shapes a different *ethos* in each case. The first way of life, Aristotle says, is not wrong, but only the second can give a person full satisfaction, as the Stagirite expects it to give fulfilment.

In the theoretical discourse, which, according to Aristotle, is neither productive nor practical, the goal is truth, construed as knowledge of the state of affairs, and thus, in another, practical thinking perspective, it is a certain good, because it prevents pernicious decisions, founded on delusions and wrong convictions. Therefore falseness is evil, but "while of the part which is practical and intellectual the good state is truth in agreement with right desire".[3] It turns out, though, that not only theoretical study leads to truth. There are more ways to reach it. In *Nicomachean Ethics* Aristotle enumerates five durable dispositions allowing humans to learn the truth (i.e. to state something or deny something): (1) scientific knowledge, (2) art (technical skills), (3) practical wisdom, (4) philosophic wisdom, (5) intuitive reason. In *Analytics*, in turn, he mentions six dispositions arranged in counterpart pairs: discursive and intuitive thinking, scientific knowledge and technical skills, practical and philosophic wisdom.[4]

What is scientific knowledge then? What does it concern? Aristotle says:

---

with Introduction and Notes by Lesley Brown, Oxford University Press, New York 2009.
3   Aristotle, *Nicomachean Ethics*, p. 103.
4   Aristotle, *Posterior Analytics*, trans. by Jonathan Barnes, Oxford University Press, Oxford 1994, [89 b 7]. Cf. Aristotle, *Nicomachean Ethics*, book VI, p. 104.

> Now what *scientific knowledge* is, if we are to speak exactly and not follow mere
> similarities, is plain from what follows. We all suppose that what we know is
> not even capable of being otherwise; of things capable of being otherwise we do
> not know, when they have passed outside our observation, whether they exist
> or not. Therefore the object of scientific knowledge is of necessity. Therefore it
> is eternal; for things that are of necessity in the unqualified sense are all eternal;
> and things that are eternal are ungenerated and imperishable. Again, every sci-
> ence is thought to be capable of being taught, and its object of being learnt. And
> all teaching starts from what is already known, as we maintain in the *Analytics*
> also; for it proceeds sometimes through induction and sometimes by deduction.
> [...] Scientific knowledge is, then, a state of capacity to demonstrate, and has the
> other limiting characteristics which we specify in the *Analytics*; for it is when a
> man believes in a certain way and the starting-points are known to him that he
> has scientific knowledge, since if they are not better known to him than the con-
> clusion, he will have his knowledge only incidentally.[5]

Only things that cannot be otherwise, are objects of pure, contemplative, knowledge. Things that can be otherwise, are divided by Aristotle into
two categories: objects of production and objects of activity, belonging respectively to the realms of *poiesis* and *praxis*.[6] People who are active in a
practical sphere, are attributed with *prudence* (*phronesis*):

> Now it is thought to be a mark of a man of practical wisdom to be able to delib-
> erate well about what is good and expedient for himself, not in some particular
> respect, e.g. about what sorts of thing conduce to health or to strength, but about
> what sorts of thing conduce to the good life in general.[7]

Poiesis, in turn, is an area of activity where the cognitive moment
materialises in rules or recipes: it is a knowledge to execute, bring into
life.[8] Therefore the knowledge of prudence can neither be scientific knowledge, nor art: it cannot be scientific, because it refers to things that can
be otherwise; on the other hand, it cannot be art, because prudence acts

---

5   Aristotle, *Nicomachean Ethics*, pp. 104-105.
6   In Book VI [1140a] he sets these forms of activity in opposition, „for neither is
    acting making nor is making acting.", and sees production as one of the arts,
    that is *techne*. Cf. Aristotle, *Nicomachean Ethics*, p. 105.
7   Aristotle, *Nicomachean Ethics*, pp. 105-106.
8   Let this enumeration testify how far *poiesis* differs from modern terms describing
    productive activity: Routine, technology, art, procedure, methodology, strategy,
    all of which is entirely contained in *poiesis*.

accordingly to the situation as opposed to acting by rules. Prudence, responsible for proper reasoning, is practical wisdom, "is concerned with things human and things about which it is possible to deliberate", which can and should be improved, in which the moment of a rational decision is essential, within boundaries separating *praxis* from *poiesis* and scientific knowledge (*episteme*).

Such a division in the area of relations between thinking and learning on the one hand, and acting and making on the other hand, is not completely transparent to us, since it reflects the social practices of then and the status of practical thinking in Aristotle's era. It does not occur to Aristotle to regulate this diversity so that prudence would be assigned functions and purposes determining the place of practical knowledge within science. He does not give it the roles of "what is capable of being taught" and "what is capable of being learnt". He lacks both the reflective Cartesian view, based on the universal point of subjective self, and the view objectivising the sphere of "what is capable of being otherwise", in a way different from the intention imposed by *poiesis*, the intention of objectivising activity in the form of a thing-product.

Aristotle always construes *praxis* as already profoundly transformed by human activity, as an environment of human existence, structured by this activity, an environment that can be entered not by a rule or recipe, not by contemplation, still less a method, but practically, that is, using prudence. The latter builds knowledge that is unsure, ephemeral, biased, non-universal, but efficient in dealing with people. In consequence "shortcomings" of theoretical thinking in the area filled with *praxis* allow to avoid epistemological problems related to reflexivity of knowledge which addresses the *ego cogito*, but at the same time, they indicate the ontic entrapment of Aristotle's thought.

In Aristotle's practical philosophy, the study of social life had its place in diverse, pluralistically construed field of knowledge. It formed without the coercion of correct reasoning or the supervision of epistemological requirements of sure knowledge, based on the foundation of unquestionable convictions leading to universally valid statements. Its purpose was to learn procedures/activities and at the same time it is in charge of procedures/activities. Therefore it is responsible for recognising, analysis and justifying the objectives of human activity, accompanied by awareness of the finite character of all human abilities and unsure efficiency of human activity. However non-contemplative, it is science. Aristotle says that one can give a general judgement about activity or conduct, but it must be remembered that it is about activity (about its specific circumstances), about what is right to do, and that by investigating that activity we change ourselves too.

Aristotle's contemporary commentators,[9] both philosophy historians and philosophers referring to selected threads of his philosophy, agree on the fact that the difference between *praxis* and *poiesis*, between doing and making, is not as clear as it may seem at the first glance. Such an opinion is supported not only by the character of Aristotle's legacy, but also the presumably inevitable, in view of over two thousand years' that have elapsed, pressure of the present, leading interpreters to more or less carefree theoretical paraphrases of his thoughts, including the penchant for presentism. Within the latter we can see overlooking the onto-epistemological motivation of Aristotle's verdicts in all those comments whose authors have gone through the school of modern epistemocentrism.[10]

---

9   Cf. Hannah Arendt, *The Human Condition*, University of Chicago Press, Chicago 1998; Tadeusz Kwiatkowski, *Poznanie naukowe u Arystotelesa. Niektóre poglądy teoretyczne (Scientific Study in Aristotle's Thought)*, PWN, Warszawa 1969; Jerzy Kalinowski, *Teoria poznania praktycznego (Theory of Practical Knowledge)*, Towarzystwo Naukowe Katolickiego Uniwersytetu Lubelskiego, Lublin 1960; Eric Voegelin, *Aristotle, Order and History*, vol. 3, *Plato and Aristotle,* The Collected Works of Eric Voegelin, vol. 16, ed. Dante Germino, University of Missouri Press, Columbia 2000, pp. 325-428.

10 „Epistemocentrism" is Pierre Bourdieu's term describing the domination of epistemology in philosophy and science, along with the consequent *"theoretical or intellectual »bias«"*, which depends on the failure to acknowledge the fact that a theory of social life being constructed by a thinker is a result of the theoretical manner of perception, a product of a "contemplative" lookout (*theorein*). In other words, Bourdieu calls epistemocentrism "a scientists' »ethnocentrism«, which entails disregard for anything that analysts project on their perception of the object for the reason of looking at it from afar and above", Pierre Bourdieu and Loïc J. D. Waquant, *An Invitation to Reflexive Sociology*, Polity Press in association with Blackwell Publishers, The University of Chicago 1992, pp. 69-70. Therefore epistemocentrism is an intellectual stance or just an intellectual habit rooted in the domain of experiences available and most often dominant

In his "Teoria poznania praktycznego"[11] ("Theory of Practical Knowledge") Jerzy Kalinowski points at certain interpretative problems in distinguishing between practical and productive knowledge. Although Aristotle distinguished these notions (*poiesis* and *praxis*), he was not consistent in their usage. The difference between conduct (*praxis*) and production (*poiesis*), in other words, doing and making, in his practical philosophy depends firstly on the fact that in the case of making (whether conduct or not) we obtain a product external in relation to the actor/producer, "undertaken with regard to something and executed accordingly".[12] Secondly, the purpose of making is something external in relation to the maker, while the purpose of conduct is the one who acts. Another difference is that "making is activity »shaping the external matter«, while "conduct lies within the active individual", which can be understood in such a way that the purpose of conduct is conduct itself.[13] It turns out that the clarity of the dichotomic division is disrupted by a special kind of human activity, highlighted by Aristotle in the area of *poiesis*, which is *techne* (art, craft). A certain characteristic links it to *praxis*: knowledge, as a component of both, involves rules. To make according to rules is to produce within *techne* (art), whereas to act means nothing else than to behave by rules. Although the rules of conduct and production are not identical, in both cases they separate *praxis* and *techne* from productive activity, which stays in the area of *poiesis*, undertaken spontaneously, as an act of involving a talent etc.

It seems that all these differences, especially the latter two, boil down to the fact that in the case of conduct we have to do with an achievement in the form of action itself. It is about doing and its autotelic meaning, while in the case of making it is about the external result of the action, external

---

in the scholars' community. Its characteristic trait is exposing the intellectual, especially cognitive, moment in all forms of human activity.

11 Cf. Kalinowski, *Teoria poznania praktycznego*, pp. 10-32. Cf. also: Andrzej Siemianowski, *Poznawcze i praktyczne funkcje nauk empirycznych (Cognitive and Practical Functions of Empirical Sciences)*, PWN, Warszawa 1976, pp. 58-78.

12 Kalinowski, *Teoria poznania praktycznego*, p. 12.

13 Kalinowski, *Teoria poznania praktycznego*, pp. 12-13.

from the maker and from the making as such (the action). In *Metaphysics*, Aristotle says:

> For in the case of things produced the principle of motion (either mind or art or some kind of potency) is in the producer; and in the case of things done the will is the agent-for the thing done and the thing willed are the same.[14]

But does Aristotle distinctly separate doing (conduct) and making? Or does he rather treat them interchangeably and reduce them to one: action? According to Kalinowski, Aristotle does not give a clear answer to the question of the mutual relation between conduct and production. Those three kinds of human activity: contemplation, behaviour and production, are sometimes reduced by Aristotle to two: contemplation and action, and knowledge is reduced to theoretical and practical activity, perhaps according to the pattern of lifestyles: *bios theoretikos* and *bios praktikos*. "After all the base for distinguishing kinds of knowledge are life activities, directly it is the purpose of acquiring knowledge, which is: in case of theoretical knowledge the study of reality itself, in case of practical knowledge guidance to right conduct, and in case of poietic knowledge, analogous guidance to making things".[15] The criterion of purpose is combined with the criterion of the sort of object, because it is not about "the subjective purpose of the investigating individual", but "the objective purpose of investigation itself".[16] At the same time, the purpose of theoretical knowledge is learning the truth. The object of practical knowledge is conduct, the purpose is guidance to right conduct.[17]

Two aspects of Kalinowski's interpretation deserve attention. Firstly, Kalinowski reduces Aristotle's pluralism in a certain epistemic or epistemological way, assuming that the intellectual moment, which, in the latter's view, is involved in every human activity, always has a cognitive

---

14 Aristotle, *Metaphysics*, book 6, section 1025 b, in: Aristotle, Aristotle in 23 Volumes, Vols. 17, 18, trans. by Hugh Tredennick, Cambridge, MA, Harvard University Press; London, William Heinemann Ltd. 1933, 1989.

15 Kalinowski, *Teoria poznania* praktycznego, p. 14.

16 Kalinowski, *Teoria poznania* praktycznego, p. 15.

17 Bear in mind that Aristotle knew the rules and principles of a doctor's job. As Nicomachus's son, trained by him in the profession, he must have recognised the connection between *ethos* and *techne*, and possibly even *episteme*.

character. Hence the ability to place all kinds of human activities in one plane of theoretical, practical and poietic knowledge, so that they constitute a complete and uniform whole of human intellectual powers, whose meaning is entirely contained in cognitive activity. Thanks to that assumption the difference between *poiesis* and *techne* can be deemed epistemically insignificant, while, from another point of view, the intellectual contribution of talent and that of an intersubjectively available principle, elaborated socially (as in case of *techne* and *poiesis*) has an altogether different character. Poietic knowledge, in Kalinowski's opinion, is part of practical knowledge, because it is also about guidance to conduct, and precisely that concerning producing a work of art. This is what rules are for, principles of, say, constructing a plot, that is "making" a tragedy or a comedy. He writes:

> For Aristotle practical knowledge in a broad sense (the same applies, *mutatis mutandis*, to practical philosophy *sensu largo*) is knowledge concerning what medieval thinkers will give a Latin name of *operabile*, that is conduct and production.[18]

This other point of view, mentioned above, lets us see an ontically relevant difference in one that is epistemologically irrelevant. For where choices motivated by universally accepted rules of knowledge are identified with choices of good for everyone, all limitations of historical time are nullified and the significance of social coercion as relevant moments of these choices are questioned. Things that "can be otherwise", so those which at least potentially remain within the area of human activity, ontically and pragmatically are not the same as "things that cannot be otherwise". On the other hand, also varieties of human activity in those two spheres of being, activities of studying, doing and making, are bound to differ according to how the agents are socially situated. Thus the difference unfolds where it is necessary to step outside the purely cognitive meaning of these activities, and then the two ways of living, *bios theoretikos* and *bios praktikos*, reveal their mutually irreducible natures. According to Aristotle a mind of studious disposition can reach where no practice or productive action has anything to do. This is not only, to use modern language, for technical reasons, but due to circumstances (*resp.* for social

---

18 Kalinowski, *Teoria poznania praktycznego*, p. 25.

reasons). Indeed, if all intellectual activity were reducible to study, the difference between *bios theoretikos* and *bios praktikos* would not be worth his attention. On the other hand, *nolens volens*, the interest in the cosmic universality of things that cannot be otherwise, is utterly alien to him in the area of human affairs.[19] The premise that he does not express, as it is obvious in his thought, is not only the pluralism of knowledge, but also cultural and social particularism. In effect, epistemological verdicts are preceded here with ontic presuppositions.

In the language of modern philosophy this premise assumes the following form: being, in its historic and social concreteness, becomes a factor motivating a respective, that is, theoretical or technical, sort of intellectual work in a specific area of that being. In consequence cognition takes part in each of these sorts of work in a different way, unable to contain the whole of intellectual activity.

Secondly, Kalinowski has a consistent inclination to reduce Aristotle's trichotomy to the modern dichotomy: practice – theory. This reduction entails reducing the intellectual moment of every activity that is not-purely-cognitive (*poiesis, praxis*) to application of theory in practice. We can see that if we rule the difference between *praxis* and *poiesis* out of the trichotomic pattern, application will be the factor connecting them. *Praxis* and *poiesis* do not differ in the function of the intellectual factor present in them.

In contrast to that, thinking of practice as application of theory, on the grounds of *praxis*, especially the idea of applying social theory in practice, is an idea thoroughly modern. In Aristotle's concepts contemplatively elaborated rules concerning objects that cannot be otherwise, are of no particular use. Their objects, in accordance with the threefold division of knowledge, are out of reach for *praxis* and *poiesis*.

The anachronism of Kalinowski's thought is a result of submission to the influence of the history of ideas shaped by modern intellectual culture, for the price of recognising epistemology as the first philosophy. The modern universalism of science brought to life by technology reduces the

---

19 So it is despite Aristotle knew the idea that expressed that parallelism, the Democritean idea of correspondence between micro- and macrocosm.

tension between *poiesis* and *praxis*, thus eliminating it as a subject of philosophical considerations. This tension, preserved in an unreduced form in Aristotle's thought, shows different kinds of relations between thought and being in a poietic relation (thought – object) and in a practical one (thought – subject).[20] This dualism hides not only the expressed philosophy that has rendered significance to the trichotomy of knowledge, but also a tacit ontological thought which by default enforces placing a producing subject and an acting subject in a bounded and already diversified space of social being.

In his lectures on social philosophy, Marek Siemek interprets *poiesis* and *praxis* in different contexts of ideas: *poiesis* as instrumental activity and *praxis* as "acting in the proper sense", autotelic activity.[21] In his words, for Aristotle proper *poiesis* is crafts, handiwork, but also art, since *techne* is a kind of skill or brilliance.[22] *Poiesis*, according to Siemek, can be translated to Habermas's instrumental activity or Weber's *Zweckrationalität*, which can be understood as purposeful and rational activity. *Praxis*, in turn, for Habermas would be communicative activity.[23] Siemek says:

> On the side of *praxis* we also have, most importantly, the whole domain of subjectivity, which is fulfilled in symbolic communication, thus, intermediated through language, through word, speech, conversation and dialogue. On the other hand, rationality of activities of poietic structure could be justifiably described, referring to the nowadays fashionable terms, as monological rationality.[24]

---

20 This issue is radically construed by Arendt: „In acting and speaking, men show who they are, reveal actively their unique personal identities and thus make their appearance in the human world, while their physical identities appear without any activity of their own in the unique shape of the body and sound of the voice. This disclosure of "who" in contra distinction to "what" somebody is–his qualities, gifts, talents, and shortcomings, which he may display or hide–sis implicit in everything somebody says and does." Arendt, *The Human Condition*, p. 179.

21 Cf. Marek J. Siemek, *Wykłady z filozofii nowoczesności (Lectures on the Philosophy of Modernity)*, Wydawnictwo Naukowe PWN, Warszawa 2012, pp. 3-21.

22 Siemek, *Wykłady z filozofii nowoczesności*, p. 10.

23 Cf. Siemek, *Wykłady z filozofii nowoczesności*, pp. 12-13.

24 Siemek, *Wykłady z filozofii nowoczesności*, p. 14.

The double opposition: the symbolic against the material and the monological against dialogical (communicative) human activity lets us keep the notion of rationality as precedent and critical in relation to the order of activity, and at the same time allowing its differentiation through the duality *praxis – poiesis*. However, when Siemek treats instrumentality as the basic characteristic of *poiesis*, it seems he commits a modernist anachronism, in such a sense, in which critique of instrumental mind is a product of modern thought. Siemek writes about *poiesis* as production, but exclusively material or technological production, which is intermediated, it constructs a world of artefacts.[25] For example, there would be no place here for Aristotle's *techne rhetorike*, which despite being instrumental activity and also communicative and symbolic, it lies in the area of *poiesis*, and more precisely, the art of making – *techne*, not *praxis*.

If *poiesis* were to be limited to modern technology (*techne*), they would be the same. The question must be asked, though, whether in the spirit of Aristotle's philosophy it can be done. Whether it can be done in compliance with the social practices of the world Aristotle lived in, whether it fits in the then existing ways of thinking.

It seems that modern people cannot imagine productive activity without designating, as its essence, the instrumental moment, the technical intermediation. Nor can we imagine a different function of operations on signs than as conveying thoughts: the function of representation, expression and communication. The boundary between "causative activity" and "regulating activity"[26] always re-emerges in the modern mind where objects of that intermediated activity show their heteronomy with respect to criteria of activity rationality. These do not allow to identify operations on signs with operations on things and enforce critical attitude to the results of technical or instrumental manipulation of interaction orders. Representation and technological production are based on different intelligibility models. Those can be separated analytically, but practically and technologically constantly interfere. Mediation plays a principal, yet

---

25 Cf. Siemek, *Wykłady z filozofii nowoczesności*, p. 10.
26 On this subject compare Marcin Czerwiński, *Kultura i jej badanie (Culture and its Study)*, Zakład Narodowy im. Ossolińskich, Wrocław 1985.

non-identical, role. The source of this kind of divisions, the source of their modern problematisation, is the modern situation of a thinking, acting and producing subject. This subject, driven by rational premises in order to effectively produce, must ceaselessly separate action on symbols from action on objects and, at the same time, in order to act, has to combine the medium of pure interaction sign with the medium of material production tool in concrete execution.

The root of Siemek's anachronism can be found then in the modern division between symbolic and material culture, as well as in the no less modern division between purposeful activity and instrumental activity. These divisions acquire meaning no earlier than in modern criticism addressed at its modern object, which is the Western post-industrial society. On the one hand, observance of the boundary between symbolic and material culture refers to the conditions of thought shaped by the disenchantment of the world. To confuse things with their symbols means to linger in the traditionally, that is, outdatedly, formed conditions of magical thinking. This way of thinking blocks all rational technological innovation, which is limited by traditional transfer of knowledge.[27] On the other hand, to understand the technological efficiency of modern science means to treat results of technology as materialisation of theory, which can be expressed with abstract symbolic means. In order to understand modern technology, to spark its potential, one must analytically separate *modi operandi* valid in the symbolic sphere and in the technological sphere, and combine them again (outside the influence of tradition, rationally) through application. Not to see the opposition of purposeful, rational human activity and purely instrumental activity means to fail to understand the modern rejection of teleology on the base of natural science, as well as to surrender without objection to the social effects of human environment transformed by technology.

Remember that the renewing of the relation between theoretical knowledge with technical practice[28] had its modern institutional origin.

---

27 The form of this transfer by default contradicts innovation, since the traditional transfer is characterised either by non-reflectiveness or hermeticity.
28 I am using the term „renewing", because I mean not yet well-recognised relations of theory and technology in ancient science. The latest discoveries and research show their deep and refined links in astronomy. Particularly significant was the

The founding of the Royal Society of London (1662), whose idea was contacting discoverers with inventors and entrepreneurs, and the later emergence of other academies of sciences and skills, was an event shaping the new face of knowledge and technology in the form of both a scientific society and a technology fair.

In Aristotle's understanding, though, *poiesis* is more than just instrumental activity. It is bringing to life, making something exist thanks to imposing form on a material base, form is already present in each being's and each activity's *entelechy*.

Therefore, also the second boundary known from ancient philosophy, that between theoretical knowledge (*episteme*) and art (*techne*), gets blurred in the modern era. It is because all production known today as technology, is subject to ever more scientifically precise and standardised (thus permanent) rules, algorithms and principles drawn from constantly confirmed mechanistic determinism. So construed causality eschews moral, aesthetic and political (practical) assessment, as it is the law of nature that governs it. The status of "poietics" was reduced to that of poetics, and *techne* split into technology and art in the modern meaning, bound with aesthetic values. Since then the ancient principles, like that calling "first of all do no wrong" in poietics, in its professional action (*primum non nocere* as a universal principle) have already had a purely ethical form: "do no harm" (while each craftsperson, politician and neighbour can do wrong). Different forms of activity connected with all kinds of production and conduct have been separated here.

The more tight the relation between technology and science becomes, the more visible it is that "conduct", social, economic and political activities are not subject to the same principles as production, as it depends on variable and contingent rules of social life, from moral order and people's will, as opposed to applying irrefutable laws of nature discovered by natural sciences. On the other hand, the more this connection shapes

---

discovery and examination of the so-called Antikythera mechanism. Cf. Tony Freeth et al., *Decoding the Antikythera Mechanism: Investigation of an Ancient Astronomical Calculator*, „Nature" 2006, vol. 444, Issue 7119, pp. 587-591.

modernity, to the greater degree modern thought strives to make this connection universal.

To follow a different route, we can observe that practice differs from technological production in yet other two significant aspects. Firstly, activity (in the sense of *praxis*) is formed directly, as opposed to production. The conditions of production and production itself have become "laboratory-like", that is intermediated by tools, machines, out of social context and being products of past technology feats. They are also distinct in being alienated from the context of traditional symbolic culture, as in order to obtain the same product the same procedures of manufacturing must be preserved, while the same principles of social life or the same moral standards or literary accounts do not. Of course, technology changes social life, principles governing it, or even moral standards, which we are witnessing especially today. It happens wherever technology steps vigorously into direct interpersonal relations.[29] Talking about the cultural neutrality I mean in the first place the very production and possibility to make a specific product, not interactions with the social environment. These obviously take place and have their non-technological consequences.

Secondly, strident secularisation processes in Western societies, those which have created new configurations of technology and science, are accompanied by the rapidly waning conviction of permanence and causative (almost technological) force of social (*resp.* "moral") life principles, sanctioned in divine order, transcending the earthly reality. As a result, the contrast between the contingency of "moral law" and the coercion of laws regarding "starry heavens" has become not only easily recognisable, but also has provoked troublesome questions about the epistemological status of the knowledge of social life. Does its practical character free it from the rigours and standards of sure knowledge? Can results obtained through investigation of nature be effective in the area of human matters? These questions have lost nothing of their acuity.

Here we can risk drawing the first conclusions.

While in the antiquity the boundary between *poiesis* and *praxis* could be blurred, because "makers" (*resp.* craftspeople) constituted a certain

---

29 Cf. Manuel Castells, *Rise of the Network Society*, Wiley-Blackwell, Oxford 1996.

political force (group of "activists"), while the medieval thought was not fully aware of it, since the arts and crafts had fallen along with Rome, and Aristotle was considered an ethician keeping away from crafts, in the early modernity the unclear distinction became a well-defined problem for thinkers. It is not only because of the utterly new pattern of knowledge participating in "practice" and "art", but also because of social roots of these new concepts. Namely, production becomes an area of developing technology with the growing influence of theoretical knowledge. It is thanks to the dazzling achievements of physics, especially mechanics, that the ever since impetuous process, based on the positive feedback between scientific knowledge and technology, had gained momentum. As a result, an invention has become equal to a theoretical discovery in social status.[30] Transferred into the area of activity, it changes the way things are made and organises people differently.

"Late modern" or "post-modern" thought, does not stray from the path of criticism. It just shifts, so to speak, the direction of the critical thought vector towards modernity itself. We have to do with a new conceptualisation of the *praxis – techne* relation and an equally new one of the relation between a sign (language) and an object. Some verdicts in this area are no longer treated as given *a priori*, enforced by a certain intellectual tradition, or necessary conditions of meaningful or rational considerations, but as problematic themselves. So emerges a new view of the complex: *techne – praxis – episteme.*[31] Among late 20th-century thinkers Foucault is prominent with his *Order of Things*: he grasps the Weberian disenchantment (*die Entzauberung*), as a principle of modernity, in a historical and critical

---

30 However this equalisation process has lasted a long time, which is demonstrated for example by the invention of a spring clock. Cf. Robert King Merton, *Science and Economy of 17th century England*, in: *Social Theory and Social Structure*, The Free Press, New York 1968, pp. 641-663. Thomas Alva Edison as a scholar and inventor is also a good example of rising hopes to shorten the way from theory to practice.

31 Cf. Ewa Bińczyk, *Technonauka w społeczeństwie ryzyka. Filozofia wobec niepożądanych następstw praktycznego sukcesu nauki (Technoscience in Risk Society. Philosophy in the Face of Undesired Consequences of Science's Practical Success)*, Wydawnictwo Naukowe UMK, Toruń 2012.

way, as an epistemic, i.e. contingent, principle of knowledge in human sciences.[32] Habermas's critique of ideologies also must be reminded here.[33]

Against this very background of ideas, the background of criticism directed at modernity itself, also epistemocentrism, which used to be an unquestioned foundation for modern criticism, loses its position as a fixed reference. This yields returning ontological conceptualisations of social sciences, at least within philosophical thought. It has become quite obvious that epistemocentrism rests on the grounds of weakening modern convictions about existential descriptions of subjectivity. "I think therefore I am" provokes resistance from many sides and almost inevitably leads to some ontological "clinamen" of thought.

In this light, onto-epistemological threads in Aristotle's philosophy reveal their significance as a certain tradition in understanding the specific subject of social sciences, which is human activity, activity that influences the shape of society. In this tradition, activities are always construed as having a definite future horizon. Prospection is inscribed in them in an indispensable way. They refer to the future and possibilities of shaping it, hence social sciences effectively do not depend on insight, but they seek intellectual forms of expression. They seek not so much the objective and the substantial, as the social and the dynamic. No wonder then that they are involved in their subject, they "deliberate" on it themselves. Social sciences in Aristotle's system aim not only to learn about conduct, but also to direct it, reaching for values. Here we come across an onto-epistemological lead taken up again in our times: social theory is not just insight into some corner of the world, but, more than anything, activity. In Charles Taylor and Bourdieu's language, social theory is also practice: it both determines the meaning and shapes activity. Involvement is not a limitation here, but liberation of the studying mind.

---

32 Cf. Michel Foucault, *The Order of Things: An Archaeology of the Human Sciences*, Routledge, London, New York 2002.

33 Cf. Andrzej M. Kaniowski, *Filozofia społeczna Jürgena Habermasa. W poszukiwaniu jedności teorii i praktyki*, (*Jürgen Habermas's Social Philosophy. In Search of Unity of Theory and Practice*), Kolegium Otryckie, Warszawa ca 1990, pp. 354-382.

Aristotle, as it seems, was aware of it. The times when he lived, the social practices of then directly shaped views and social theories. And it was not a subversive opinion, either in Aristotelian pluralism of knowledge, or in the democratic *polis*. Yet according to Aurelius Augustine and his follower it already verged on heresy. Radical changes in approach to society as a subject of science, though, were to come only in the early modern times.

Charles Taylor calls Aristotle's model of knowledge a participational model[34] and he puts it in opposition to the modern model, which he calls, in turn, a representational one. In Aristotle's philosophy to study means, according to Taylor, to participate conceptually in the essence (*eidos*) of what is studied. The mind, which is formed by the very *eidos*, participates in the studied object's being, as opposed to simply representing it. Knowledge is not observation detached from action and opposing it as a different modality, it is not a biased, idiosyncratic vision of something that exists in itself. Knowledge is activity itself, one of its types, it is participation, not mapping. Hans-Georg Gadamer, whose opinions Taylor often leans on, puts it like this:

> As people we are also people among people, social beings, and only departing from that practice of being human, one or another can turn, from time to time, for a moment, towards pure knowledge.[35]

2. The unitary model of knowledge: Descartes

One of the most influential images in the history of knowledge is the metaphor of knowledge as a tree.[36] The archaic or even archetypal roots of this image are confirmed by its semantic polyvalence. Its diverse moral,

34 Cf. Charles Taylor, *Overcoming Epistemology*, in: Charles Taylor, *Philosophical Arguments*, Harvard University Press, Cambridge, London 1995, p. 3.
35 Hans-Georg Gadamer, *Pochwała teorii (Praise of Theory)*, in: Hans-Georg Gadamer, *Teoria, etyka, edukacja. Eseje wybrane (Theory, Ethics, Education. Selected Essays)*, ed. Paweł Dybel, Wydawnictwo Uniwersytetu Warszawskiego, Warszawa 2008, p. 37.
36 Cf. Manuel Lima, *The Book of Trees: Visualizing Branches of Knowledge*, Princeton Architectural Press, New York 2014.

hermetic, epistemic, religious applications have inhabited the world for many centuries. The Cartesian version of this image is as follows:

> Philosophy as a whole is like a tree; of which the roots are Metaphysics, the trunk is Physics, and the branches emerging from this trunk are all the other branches of knowledge. These branches can be reduced to three principal ones, namely, Medicine, Mechanics, and Ethics (by which I mean the highest and most perfect Ethics, which presupposes a complete knowledge of the other branches of knowledge and is the final stage of Wisdom).[37]

This is a model of knowledge that can be called unitary. Not only does it forge a conviction of human knowledge's common roots, but it also harbours a fundamentalist inspiration: the tree of knowledge is firmly rooted in its environment and it can grow because its construction is based on *fundamentum inconcussum*, an irrefutable basis. As we know, this basis is the *Cogito*'s self-consciousness, or, as it has been construed since Kant, the pre-reflective (non-intentional) awareness of performing an act of consciousness directed at an object. Hence the knowledge-tree model is also his model of epistemology, as fundamentalist as that of Descartes.[38]

> In Descartes's thought, the notion of order is linked with the vision of knowledge's organic unity. It is expressed in the organic metaphor of a tree, which was present also in Llull's concept. This metaphor depicts a network-like, knot-like model of unified knowledge. So conceived knowledge is supposed to mirror the very structure of the world and provide an essentialist map of the nature of all things. The image of a tree, however drawing attention to fruit symbolising practical benefits for the human kind, instead of the traditional philosophy's speculation, also incorporates metaphysics as the roots of the tree. Its importance, despite it is not an objective in itself, lies in being an indispensable means to an end, which is reaching practical and sure philosophical knowledge. Metaphysics provides stability of Cartesian knowledge system, since it allows to formulate philosophical foundations of links in this network, which justify this system as a whole.[39]

---

37 René Descartes, *Principles of Philosophy*, translated with explanatory notes, by Valentine Rodger Miller and Reese P. Miller, Kluwer Academic Publishers Dordrecht, Boston, London 1992, p. XIV.

38 This issue is properly captured by Małgorzata Czarnocka. Cf. Małgorzata Czarnocka, *Podmiot poznania a nauka* (*The Knowing Subject and Science*), Monografie Fundacji na rzecz Nauki Polskiej, Wrocław 2003, pp. 22-30.

39 Joanna Judycka, *Paralelizm strukturalny projektów nauki uniwersalnej Lulla i Kartezjusza (Structural Parallelism of Llull's and Descartes's Projects of Universal Science)*, „Filo-Sofija" 2013, no. 22, p. 224.

Criticism of this model of epistemology and the model's significance for sciences and philosophy were growing as modern thought was conceptualising the place of science and philosophy in social reality, but also parallelly with the scientific conceptualisation of this reality. It was social sciences that expressed criticism and possible improvement programmes within the school of thought overtly or implicitly admitting to the Cartesian legacy. That justifies the statement that nothing unproblematic has left of that legacy. Epistemological fundamentalism, representationism, substantialism in understanding a subject, naturalism and evolutionism in understanding science, ahistoricism in understanding thought: these are only the main strands of René Descartes's philosophy which have been debated thoroughly enough, both in the form of multi-faceted critique and attempts to delve into their philosophical subtleties. Here, though, we are only interested in a quite narrow aspect of Cartesianism: its role in social sciences as a residual, reduced onto-epistemology.

The Cartesian onto-epistemology has a completely different form than the one pervading Aristotle's knowledge pluralism. The reason for that is the identification of *fundamentum inconcussum* with a specifically (metaphysically) construed thought, substantialised as a subject-*Cogito*. His or her being is identical with a thought-act, which fulfils that being only in cognition, in intentional "lean" towards an object. Yet there is a certain flaw in the epistemological connection between the thought-being and the thought-intentional act: self-knowledge could be considered equivalent to acknowledgement of being, just because it does not have a nature of an act. Immanence is always more certain than transcendence towards something. That is why to think and to be is the same. Of course, only for a *subiectum*, for *Cogito*. Being and acknowledgement of being blend into one substantial whole, whereas objective knowledge is a kind that always lacks this acknowledgement and it is always problematic exactly because it has a nature of an act, that is, it "reaches" for something that it is not.

Descartes, using his philosophy, achieved a radical rearrangement of the image of knowledge order known since Aristotle. He gave it an utterly different form, a fundamentalist and uniform one, which that philosophy did not have to pay for, as the cost depended on narrowing the idea of scientific investigation and philosophical self-investigation by shedding social sciences. Since in Aristotle's model, they formed part of practical and technological knowledge, they could be separated from the domain of study that deserves epistemological debate, with a simple gesture identifying sure knowledge (*episteme*). "Temporary ethics" is a common name for all forms of knowledge about the human being, worth mentioning only for practical requirements. This omission, seemingly inevitable for Descartes's fundamentalism, only much later revealed its weight. For the first time, we could see that in Kant's work, in his considerations of the place of anthropology on the knowledge order.

Descartes's separation of knowledge and custom, reading and observation, theoretical, methodical, and critical reflection from practical and technological thought, valuable knowledge and opinions, is most clearly visible in his neglect of ethical knowledge. His temporary ethics is not compliant with the conditions he imposes on scientific knowledge. In fact, his improvement project concerning philosophy reached much farther. Using the prior divisions, we may say that Descartes performed two operations in that matter: identifying *praxis* with *poiesis* in their cognitive functions, which they could have in the environment of being in the world, and subjugating them to scientific knowledge, based on the self-conscious *Cogito*. Descartes follows two paths simultaneously. First, he assigns the same epistemological status of unsure knowledge, lacking foundations, to technological and practical knowledge. The differences between them, which could surface in their cognitive functions for a subject that is ontically connected with the world, disappear following the disappearance of the ontic bond between the world and the subject (*Cogito*). The substantialisation of human mental activity, which is indispensable for that severance, allows to transform people's being into "thinking-being" of a subject-substance, and set his or her being characteristics in opposition to the "world's" being characteristics.[40] Secondly, it is a change of role that Descartes attributes to knowledge in the area of merged *praxis* and *techne*. This role is an embodiment of the idea of application. It allows to understand knowledge as an area of activity completely separate in its

---

40 The evolution of the meanings of two terms: subjective and objective, is historically significant. Cf. Lorraine Daston, Peter Galison, *Objectivity*, Zone Books, New York 2007. Cf. also Chapter V, p. 2 in this book.

essence from other human achievements (practical and technological), but hugely influencing the latter. The idea of application as a form of presence of the intelligible in the instrumental-objective, reduces all differences of *techne*'s and *praxis*'s forms of intelligibility to a moment coined from the outside, from the being of *Cogito* and his/her mental activity. It has fundamental consequences for understanding how the bonds a subject-*Cogito* can create with the world are narrowed. In action it is the bond through technology, a form of intermediation always possible to reduce to *Cogito*'s intelligibility in the objective (in objects); in the sphere of aesthetic experience the bond uses intelligibility of a sign instead of the directness of similarity (*mimesis*); in the area of interpersonal relations, the intermediation is carried out through customs instead of moral intuition. All these intermediations have basically one ontic meaning: they reflect forms of *Cogito*'s presence in the world of objects as projections of the thought-*subiectum*. Intuition, a direct picture, plays its role only in reference to the pre-reflective form of *Cogito*'s self-awareness. Therefore this scheme of thought cannot overlook the ontological status of thought, that is, its incessant reference to being a *Cogito*, given indirectly, through its intelligibility forms present in the object-oriented and objective sphere of social being, as well as the direct being of thought, given in the experience of self. That is why the ontological status of thought in its intentional lean towards an object becomes all but suppressed, it is only the being of an entity captured in this lean.

In consequence, then, the role of Cartesian onto-epistemology has a twofold nature, since it involves onto-epistemological thinking in its completely different functions in the area of philosophy and in sciences. This is the fundamental achievement of Cartesianism, as long as this dualism can be construed to be the development that in early modernity paved the way for epistemological fundamentalism and substantialism in understanding a thinking subject. At the same time, it can be seen as a "metaphysical denial" to understand subjectivity in any way that is not *Cogito*-oriented. Those roots of practical sciences that had grown from social orders had to be cut off if the new meaning of scientific knowledge were to develop, with its postulates of methodical thinking and its application in the area known before, but before otherwise construed: in the area of *praxis* and *techne*.

However influential Descartes's onto-epistemology may be, in sciences it has an utterly residual significance. It is due to two mutually exclusive needs created by Descartes's metaphysical dualism. The first is the need for exploration of the self as the ontological basis, i.e. for *fundamentum inconcussum*. This basis obviously cannot be built by means available to science, since the latter must already be rooted in some ground, as suggested by the image of the knowledge tree. The second need is meeting the postulate of universal knowledge, which by default describes everything that is a being in the world. That world is given by *Cogito*'s forms of consciousness, hence in the form of something whose being is nullified as its own being in forms of presence for the studying *Cogito*. Therefore the metaphysical concept of self-knowing *Cogito* as *fundamentum inconcussum* fails to link ontological concepts of objects described by scientific knowledge. On the contrary, it withdraws all ontology to the sphere of the *Cogito*'s being and suspends the validity of the question how the world exists for scientific knowledge. This residual onto-epistemology, which forces thinking to experience itself in the sphere of *Cogito* as being and does not allow metaphysical intrusions in the area of scientifically objectivised cognitive experience, is a result of the conflict mentioned above. The experience of thought as self-presence opposes the experience of something conveyed by this thought as an object of unbiased investigation. For it is there, in the sphere of immanence, that we can see a rolling, ontologically uniform, neutral landscape of knowledge based on self-knowledge, which is not itself a result of, however construed, objective research. The latter is governed by representation and indirectness, related to signs or instrumental, social at last, as coercion of custom in moral knowledge.

Hence, wherever in the world the subjective nature of some practical or poietic human activity comes to the surface, the need emerges, as it cognitive correlates, to reduce this activity to the activity of *Cogito*. Facing the threat of that activity's dispersal as practical and technical, that is creative and causative in constructions existing only as given to that *Cogito* (not transcending the borders of immanence and ontically indeterminate), it constantly has to be "exported" to the world, hence different ways of objectivising its presence in the world must be searched for. However, the source of this activity lies in *Cogito*, absent in the world. Therefore this search must follow errant trails or accept non-scientific, unbased, metaphysical intrusions. The more this activity opens to investigation, the harder it is to place its presence in the world. The easier it is to acknowledge its consequences for being, the less it is available for study. As a result, in order to acknowledge the presence of this activity in the world, paradoxically it must be excluded from the world of *Cogito*, which is exactly what lets us investigate it and what is the source of its intelligibility.

Such is the meaning of that early modern, residual onto-epistemology in the area of social sciences: it is detachment of activity from people's being in the world and identifying it with the moment of intelligibility of being in the world. In the unitary model, the knowledge of action was reduced to the knowledge of *Cogito*, determined by its reflectivity: recognition of the intelligible moment of thought in what it is different from it. The question of whether action has an intelligibility form different from thinking, in view of the Cogito's metaphysical primacy as *fundamentum inconcussum*, could not be even posed here. Heteronomy of action as opposed to thinking is the main obstacle for onto-epistemological thinking in its Cartesian version.

How did it happen? What provided the socio-historic foundation for this radical thought? Onto-epistemology of an individual subject, of the Cartesian *Cogito*, could have been a rescue strategy against the social, political or simply cultural turmoil of early modern Europe. That is possibly what Descartes was to repeatedly return to, when systems of knowledge rooted in a specific social order crumbled. Philosophy entrenched in a place isolated from social life and armed with a system of metaphysical or epistemological separation from that life, is, for many reasons, an attractive idea, both from the philosophical and the scientific points of view. In the 20th century its deluded claims to rightfulness could be considered serious. And yet this Cartesian dominance forged intellectual conditions for social sciences' self-consciousness. That self-consciousness stands in the way of investigating what Aristotle called *praxis* and *techne*.

3. Modern sciences versus ancient sciences: Oblivion of the common foundation

Science as we understand it and we do it nowadays, assumed its preliminary, but basically modern, form in the first half of the 17th century. This

formation, along with accompanying cultural and social processes, opened
the modern era in Western culture. Moreover, modernity, in its complex
forms, is largely a civilisational consequence of changes in understanding,
treating and functioning of science. The modern ideal of science, to use the
term introduced by Stefan Amsterdamski, was radically different from one
that had prevailed before and that had already been shaped in antiquity.[41]
Before the turn of the 17th-century revolution sciences were rooted in the
context of lifeworld, of human experience. That experience participated in
social order in an utterly different way than it was to be after the 17th century. Pre-modern sciences, bound with the rigours of traditional religious
doctrine, with teaching methods shaped in closed monastic environments,
are the opposite of cultural and social ideals of participation in knowledge
which formed in modern times. Growing independence from other forms
of culture, development as an intellectual imperative, unprecedented influence on the social environment – these are only selected traits of science
formed by 17th-century revolutions.

It is also visible in purely intellectual changes in science, for example
in the way universality is seen as a significant quality of valuable knowledge. For the people of antiquity, the ideal was the notion of universality
described by Greeks as *ta mathemata*: "what one can teach and learn,
and that means that experience would thereby be neither helpful nor even

---

41 On the difference between ancient and modern sciences compare: Stefan
Amsterdamski, *Between History and Method: Disputes about the Rationality of Science*, trans. by Gene M. Moore, Olga Amsterdamska, Springer
Science+Business Media, Dordrecht 2012; Lucio Russo, *The Forgotten Revolution. How Science Was Born in 300 BC and Why It Had to Be Reborn*, trans.
Silvio Levy, Springer Verlag, Berlin, Heidelberg and New York 2004. A radical,
revolutionary change of understanding science in early modernity is an important historical argument supporting the statement that science develops through
shake-ups, rather than in a continuous, cumulative way. Cf. Paweł Bytniewski,
*Trzy modele nieciągłego procesu historii nauk - Bachelard, Canguilhem, Fou-
cault (Three Models of the Discontinuous Process of the History of Sciences
- Bachelard, Canguilhem, Foucault)*, „Filozofia i Nauka. Studia filozoficzne i
interdyscyplinarne" 2015, vol. 3, pp. 241-263.

indispensable."[42] – hence the Pythagorean primacy of, allegedly more rational, knowledge acquired outside the "agora", through individual considerations of meaning and being. What ancient Greeks deemed science, theoretical knowledge, Aristotle similarly described in *Nicomachean Ethics*: as something, a kind of knowledge "capable of being taught, and its object of being learnt", and the subjects of such knowledge were considered to be inevitable and eternal, to be "things incapable of being otherwise".[43] "Experience" was rather linked to the existential conditions of individual life, than the elementary characteristics of cognitive content that it conveys. Thus, Aristotle and his contemporaries construed science pluralistically and contextually, as I wrote before. Specific kinds of knowledge differed epistemologically, in the ways thinking was involved in them, in their objects, in their methods. However, there was an element connecting them with a substantial bond: the living environment, human matters and the place of knowledge among them. Hence the opposition of *bios theoretikos* and *bios praktikos* had, more than anything, practical meaning. It referred not so much to the epistemological difference between the sureness of self-consciousness and the insecurity of objective knowledge, as it allowed to classify two different ways of living: the way which is subjugated to cognitive activity delving into being and shaping the whole of a person's life, and the way that relegates knowledge to secondary roles, not-purely-cognitive. Despite the diversity of sciences (with respect to the subject matter, the methods, the purposes), in the ancient world, they formed a whole, expressed intentionally as "philosophy", and stemming from the common life environment, in which people could, in a specific, uniformly assessed way, find the meaning of cognitive activity and navigate their lives towards the ideal of wisdom.

That is why the emergence of *polis* was enormously significant for the rise of ancient intellectual culture. In a seminal way this kind of organisation

---

42 *Hans-Georg Gadamer on Education, Poetry, and History Applied Hermeneutics*, ed. Dieter Misgeld and Graeme Nicholson, trans. Lawrence Schmidt and Monica Reuss, State University of New York Press, Albany 1992, p. 211.

43 Cf. Aristotle, *Nicomachean Ethics*, p. 104. Cf. Mariola Kuszyk-Bytniewska, *Epistemocentrism as an Epistemological Obstacle in the Social Sciences*, „Dialogue and Univesalism" 2012, vol. 22, issue 4, pp. 17-34.

affected cultural relations, mainly through the invention of word (*logos*) openly circulating in public space, word which became an instrument of a new form of authority, that was democracy.[44] Before the ruling word functioned in the society rather like a spell, it had causal power, because its strength was connected with the speaker's strength, with their position, not with the meaning of the word itself. It was only word trained in common public space, used in arguing, in "duels", that forged conditions for rational arguments, and the *polis*, by its social order, enabled that spiritual order. The word experienced and modified in common public space became an efficient form of authority, persuasive power, force of argument, wherever balance of powers, of participation in power, property and history made the community a political entity. No wonder then that various genres of word art: rhetoric, dialectics, sophistry and philosophy, paved the way for logic, the art of proof and theoretical knowledge. It was no more a *basileus* or *genos*, depositaries of *arche* (power) and causal word, but *demos* became a force determining the rules of social and intellectual life.[45] "Knowledge, values, and mental techniques, in becoming elements of a common culture, were themselves brought to public view and submitted to criticism and controversy" [46] Dispute, argument and polemic were constituted as new rules, not just of the political game, but the intellectual one as well. In this context alphabetical script gained exceptional significance. Borrowed from the Phoenicians, enriched by the Greeks with characters for local vowels, it offered the possibility to record laws, standardised the language community (*koine*), it allowed to subvert ritual forms of thinking. The changes caused by the emergence and rapid spread of writing guaranteed stability of laws, their permanence, common recognition and communality. Lastly, they forged conditions for social circulation of intellectual ideas unknown in oral culture. The recording of

---

44 Cf. Jean-Pierre Vernant, *The Origins of Greek Thought*, Cornell University Press 1982; Pierre Vidal-Naquet, *The Black Hunter: Forms of Thought and Forms of Society in the Greek World*, Johns Hopkins University Press, 1986 and Marcel Detienne, *The Masters of Truth in Archaic Greece*, trans. Janet Lloyd, Zone Books, New York 1999.

45 Cf. Detienne, *The Masters of Truth in Archaic Greece*, pp. 89-106.

46 Vernant, *The Origins of Greek Thought*, p. 51.

the laws resulted not only in their permanence and detachment from the context of their enforcement, but also in the citizens' equality in reference to them. The writing of *Iliad* and *Odyssey* similarly regulated the *topoi* of thinking and intellectual sensitivity.

Desacralisation of political life and the formation of official religion, sanctioning the state's existence, also supported democratisation.[47] *Sophia, philosophia* began to gain ground at the expense of earlier rituals, mysticism and divination practices. Studies, proofs and arguments were to gradually take their place. All citizens of a democratic *polis* were *homoioi* (similar) and *isoi* (equal), everyone in the *polis* was alike, and therefore equal in laws and duties. *Hybris*, the unstoppable will to live, whose praise we still find in Homer's poems, is now seen as a vice, because it is *sophrosyne*, restraint, prudence, moderation that became valued in a community of the equal.[48]

Due to socio-political changes in Greece in the 7th and 6th century BC, described here shortly, a new image of the world came into being, new ideas and intellectual activity forms were born, whose meaning for the development of culture cannot be underestimated today. The slogan displayed at the entrance to Plato's Academy threatened: LET NO ONE IGNORANT OF GEOMETRY ENTER HERE! This claim is a perfect expression of bonds between practical, philosophical and political thought. The Greek reason was thus a result of actual interpersonal relations, it had social roots. Its theoretical, practical, as well as productive form, were deeply immersed in the lifeworld.[49]

---

47 Modern secularisation also significantly contributed to civilisational development. Cf. Charles Taylor, *Sources of the Self. The Making of the Modern Identity*, Harvard University Press, Cambridge, Massachusetts 1994.

48 In consequence, the old ways got replaced with ones unknown before: "What was now extolled was an austere ideal of reserve and restraint, a severe, almost ascetic way of life that obscured differences of manner and rank between citizens in order to bring them closer together, to unite them like the members of one big family." Vernant, *The Origins of Greek Thought*, pp. 64-65.

49 Reason appeared in the agora, but only because the First Supporters of Law (nature) had to face disbelief and mockery from the traditionally thinking plebs. Justification and proof are invention of theoretical, as opposed to practical, rationality. A speculative statement may be surprising or outrageous for the populace, but a proof "compels" them to accept it by the force of argument. The

The modern era with the changes that it brought, and which found their especially accurate expression in the modern ideal of science,[50] led to disintegration of the unity that had connected the knowledge known to the ancient and to oblivion of common social roots from which it had grown. According to Gadamer, severance from the background provided by the social, ethical and political habitat, led to the disintegration of the earlier holistic form of knowledge: "the emergence of the modern empirical sciences in the seventeenth century is the event in which the previous form of the totality of knowledge, of philosophy or philosophia in the broadest sense of the word, began to disintegrate."[51]

A similar view is shared by Siemek:

> So then decomposed the ancient order or ethos, in which the ethical was united with the political, in symbiosis with it as *concretum*, an ethos whose philosophical expression was the classical Greek *logos*. So disintegrated the classical Greek *praxis* of political activity, beautiful freedom as a permanent condition, not a fleeting moment and the world of make-believe, as Schiller put it. [...] a process that can be called the ultimate oblivion of philosophical mind, oblivion of its socio-dialogic roots, of its pedigree of ethical politics of classical antiquity's community, above all Greek. This politics and ethics was most comprehensively described by Aristotle in his *Politics* and his *Ethics*.[52]

The sources of the utopian hope for a universal modern science lay in the Cartesian belief in one world and one science stemming from the metaphysical core. The "divine truthfulness", a metaphysical link between the subjective sureness and the objective truth, guaranteed freedom of seeking knowledge. For ultimately the true and sure knowledge had to comply both with God's intention of creation and with the spiritual affinity of God and human being. Throughout early modernity, this utopian hope supported the struggle for universality of laws. The discussed disintegration of the ancient knowledge order resulted both in abandoning the unity

---

"beginning" discussed here is also the beginning of discourse as a new form of expression and communication, a new structure of thought and speech, different from a political speech, religious summons or a fable, a mythological narrative.

50 Cf. Amsterdamski, *The Modern Ideal of Science*, in: Amsterdamski, *Between History and Method*, pp. 44-64.

51 *Hans-Georg Gadamer on Education, Poetry, and History*, p. 212.

52 Siemek, *Wykłady z filozofii nowoczesności*, pp. 19-20, 45.

of sciences, practised in the antiquity, and in disrupting the consistency of scientific knowledge, resulting from the projection of *Cogito* onto experience. In retrospection, we can reckon these changes led to the dichotomy of human and natural sciences constituted in the 19th century. The latter duality, so characteristic to the modern order of scientific knowledge, has found a solid base in the changes taking place in modern times. Firstly, an opposition was forged between "techno-science" and social practice, since it was not possible to project the former's methodical principles onto the area of the latter. Secondly, the above-mentioned duality of sciences was strongly supported by the opposition of the sureness and directness of self-knowledge experience, and the insecurity and indirectness (especially technological intermediation) of the experience of the objective world.

In early modernity, Aristotle's division into theoretical, practical and productive sciences completely changed the meaning, created in antiquity.[53] The effect of these changes is also visible in axiological collisions – of practical and theoretical values, action and study – unknown to the ancient order of knowledge. They can be clearly seen in Descartes's work: erecting the building of sure knowledge, he locked ethics in the "outhouse" of temporary ethics. In this respect, since the scientific revolution of the 17th century, in the area of science "axiological reductionism" has been becoming binding. Amsterdamski captured it finely in the postulate: "My ethics is my methodology".[54] This encapsulates the change of axiological order. Harmonising practical values with values of knowledge ceased to be the "natural" norm of knowledge's axiological order. By giving consistent priority to values of knowledge, priority guaranteeing dominance of knowledge over action, conditions were forged for science's autonomy. On the other hand, values of knowledge were pitched against practical and technical ones.[55] *Poiesis* reduced to *techne*, siding with *episteme*, together

---

53 The immense legacy of philosophy was ordered through division and segregation. Maybe then, paradoxically, Aristotle is the culprit and the early modern retreat from Aristotelian thinking sparked efforts to integrate knowledge into *sapientia universalis*.

54 Amsterdamski, *The Sources of the Crisis of the Modern Ideal of Sciences*, in: Amsterdamski, *Between History and Method*, p. 97.

55 This is perfectly clear in medicine, where technology and science are always a step ahead of morality: first a question is posed about the scientific efficiency

shape modern science, in which *praxis* is boiled down to a residual form. It is only present in the application of science or concerns activities impossible to capture in theory because of their changeability, lack of method, moral judgement, and thus marginal for the rationality of modern science.

The results of these changes is philosophically summarised in Immanuel Kant's work. The Kantian idea of the world's unity does not fit within scientific knowledge, in spite of its regulating function in that knowledge. Hence the division of reason into theoretical and practical kinds is an expression of a mind that believes in the unified world. At the same time, it conveys yet another conviction: of the inevitable duality of human mind, and consequently of the divide between what can constitute knowledge (science) and what cannot. So, although Kant does not confront the ancient state of knowledge, his notion of reason as a faculty is undoubtedly polemic to knowledge's past. Theoretical reason marks the boundaries of research within the area of experience and creates science, whereas practical reason determines the boundaries of human being's autonomy, of freedom and ability to act. The first area encompasses natural sciences and the second is knowledge of culture. The possibility of human sciences, that is the possibility of a scientific discourse on culture, although sketched in Kant's *Anthropology,*[56] was only brought into being by his descendants.

Oblivion of the common ontic base of sciences also had that important result that in early modernity all practice (including political practice?) was reduced to technology: it has been assumed that practice is application of technology and science. The newly founded, scientifically oriented social sciences, adopted such an idea of practice, however, it is always problematic at least in view of the lack of readymade technologies, waiting to be applied. That is why frequent attempts are made to forge *ad hoc* any technology of action, or otherwise, technologies are transferred from natural sciences, although these are of no use whatsoever in social reality.[57]

---

and technical possibility of action, and only then arises a question whether it is right or wrong.

56 Immanuel Kant, *Anthropology from a Pragmatic Point of View*, trans. by Robert B. Louden, Cambridge University Press, 2006.

57 Division of labour is a good example. It is a devilishly brilliant invention: to order illiterates along the production tape so that they build a computer not having any idea of what it is.

This state of affairs is a significant cause of newly emerged empirical human sciences' failures and dead ends. At the same time, it is a motif of radical projects in the area of philosophy and sociology, in which the 20th century often sees returns to antiquity (for example Heidegger, Gadamer, Foucault, Bourdieu). Reference to the Greek concept of science gives us a meaningful lesson about the common background of knowledge, forgotten in early modernity.

First of all, it is a lesson of "the grammar of sciences", namely that "there are sciences", as opposed to "there is science": The plural form, not singular, should be consistently used here. Historical, cultural, social "inflections" of sciences and their epistemological consequences were best understood, as it seems, by French philosophers and science historians only in the 20th century.[58] Anglo-Saxon tradition of philosophy and history of science is still ignoring this fact.

Secondly, it is a lesson of a certain diversity in basic dimensions of sciences, of roles they can play in their social and cultural environment. Social sciences not only are governed by different rules than natural ones, not only their subject matter has its peculiarities, but they also serve different purposes. For they are not only about investigating certain aspects of reality; they strive to change actions that can be performed thanks to the investigation, they are about good and efficient action. Sciences then differ not just in methodology and subject matter, but in purposes as well: social sciences inevitably change the reality described by them, if only through their very presence in the social order they contribute to. Knowledge in social sciences is characterised by certain peculiar (because non-cognitive) dynamics: it does not just describe and explain, but it also affects what it describes. It is always involved in the subject.

In the name of *Cogito*'s metaphysical and epistemological priority, placing the value of knowledge above any other values, modern philosophy and science have rejected the value of pluralism in sciences and involvement in the subject of study, regardless of the price that had to be

---

58 Cf. Paweł Bytniewski, *Filozofia nauk, czyli epistemologiczne pożytki z historii poznania naukowego (Philosophy of Sciences, that is, Epistemological Advantages of History of Scientific Cognition)*, Filozofia i Nauka. Studia filozoficzne i interdyscyplinarne" 2014, vol. 2, pp. 113-134.

paid. Have any essential goals been actually achieved by this oblivion? What is the non-cognitive price of that oblivion?

It seems that one important and negative consequence of this state of affairs is overestimation of the value of knowledge in cultural orders of the Western world. When technology replaces ethics in the area of social practices and suppresses *phronesis*, the moral subject gets "blurred", the subjective aspect of agency diminishes, and it manifests in waning responsibility. We live in a world where it is easy to relegate responsibility for a person's deeds to rules, paragraphs, bureaucratic procedures, technologies, brain deficiencies, dispositions and genetic code. Contemporary *praxis* is so dependent on theoretical science and its applications, that it enforces reflective (scientific and technological) intermediation in people's image of themselves, it largely forms under the influence of an expert-oriented vision of social order. Gadamer was aware of this modern complication, when he wrote:

> The new ideal of method and the objectivity of cognition guaranteed by this method have forced knowledge, as it were, out of the context of teaching and living and driven it out of knowledge shared in language and society. They have introduced a new tension into what is meant by human knowledge and human experience.[59]
> Meanwhile, it suffices to reach, if not for ancient Aristotle, then for contemporary Gadamer, to recall the meaning of *praxis* elaborated in antiquity:
> Praxis does not merely mean acting according to rules and is not merely the application of knowledge, but means the whole original situatedness of humans in their natural and social environment.[60]

Praxis, according to Gadamer, forges a primary social bond connecting everyone living in the community. Thus, we have a question to settle: to what extent this participation in the community affects the way people see their place in the world, and to what degree this participation depends on modern, reflective and technological intermediation of relations with the social environment.

Acting together creates rules and norms of activity independently of intelligibility imposed on them by subjective reflection. When patterns of

---

59 *Hans-Georg Gadamer on Education, Poetry, and History*, p. 212.
60 Cf. *Hans-Georg Gadamer on Education, Poetry, and History*, p. 217.

behaviour become adopted and widespread, they bring expected and un-expected, required and uncalled-for results, but they get largely forgotten, removed from consciousness. In a great measure, we act unreflectively and routinely, which does not hamper the development of rationality, in-telligibility and susceptibility of actions to interpretation. Meanwhile, in creating social science about actions and their orders according to the re-flectivity model of *Cogito*, we forget that action appears to an agent along with contextual conditions of its possibility, situated outside the range of individual reflection. Group activity planted in specific conditions of life and its intersubjective nature, create the whole social world, including its foundations.

Gadamer describes our contemporary, modern situation as double citizenship:

> On the one hand, the tradition of our culture, which formed us, determines our self-understanding by means of its linguistic-conceptual structure which origi-nated in the Greek dialectic and metaphysics. On the other hand, the modern empirical sciences have transformed our world and our whole understanding of the world. The two stand side by side.[61]

By science (*episteme, mathesis*), ancient philosophy understood the whole, the sum of dispersed knowledge about the world and nature, stemming from the common background of life practices, which could be subject to problematisation and that is what they required. In one researcher-philosopher's writings one could find treatises "on everything", that is, about what was interesting, with no special selection from the point of view of methodical rigour, for example on vapours, on all things, on knowledge, on saliva, on sweat. Aristotle's *Parva Naturalia* provides many instances of this concept of knowledge (a collector's concept, by the way). From today's point of view, it was a mixture of philosophy, practical medicine, meteorology, common-sense physics and other miscel-laneous pre- and parasciences, which retained consistency thanks to that background, the context of life, its practical and theoretical requirements. Crossing epistemological thresholds between science and non-science was not perplexing enough to warrant a more specific articulation.

---

61 *Hans-Georg Gadamer on Education, Poetry, and History,* p. 213.

Since the Cartesian breakthrough, the restrictive ideal of science, sub-jugated to the value of method, has made human sciences, sciences about society, problematic. This state of affairs is largely connected not only with the changes in science's ideals, but also with different relations between theory and practice in antiquity and in modernity.

4. Theoretical versus practical sciences: The modern detachment of knowledge from action

The problem of theory's relation to practice, although familiar to Western intellectual culture since the very beginnings of autonomous theoretical thought, and therefore seemingly eternal, has its history. Here I would like to stress a crucial moment of this history, when the modern variant of this problem arose, as it is modernity that has given it a special significance for the onto-epistemological status of social sciences. Never before had theo-retical thinking, purely cognitive insight, played such an important role in modifying human life environment, and at the same time never before had relations between theory and practice become so blurred as a result of the epistemological self-awareness. The paradox of this awareness lies in the fact that the more modern forms of knowledge influenced the social reality (through technology, institutional education and science, mass media etc.), the further epistemological concepts detached knowledge from action as well as knowledge from social orders. Since the modern intellectual era gave the role of *philosophia prima* to epistemology, it has either explicitly or implicitly severed the bonds that had connected the concepts of being and study, action and knowledge.

Study (cognition), although experienced by an individual as action and sharing many characteristics with other activities, has been endowed in modern times with features allowing to see it in opposition to action. From then on, action could only be construed as a peculiar derivative of cogni-tion, adopting the intelligibility of that cognition, hidden in the agent's subjectivity and only from there radiating outwards. Action-oriented cog-nition discovered there only structures of monadic subjectivity, autono-mous in regard to the world's being, but unable to determine the being of its superindividual conditions, freed from subjectivity. So construed reflec-tivity of *Cogito* has stumbled upon repeated difficulties in understanding the role of action in shaping social bonds and possibility to join one agent's action with another one's.[62] It was the monadic character of Cartesian subjectivity that posed the main difficulty. This was certainly understood by post-phenomenological philosophers (M. Heidegger, H.-G. Gadamer, H. Arendt), but also in the area of anti-positivist sociology (F. Znaniecki, Ch. Cooley, G.H. Mead). As long as the relation between study and action was seen in epistemological categories, that is, without ontological involvement, "action" remained a category of social sciences: a fundamental one, but dependent in meaning on the act of acquiring knowledge, a derivative of cognition's intelligibility.[63] *Cogito*, rejected nowadays as an alleged factor shaping social bonds, kept returning to social sciences on the grounds of the subjective character and reflectivity of the "meaning" of action. Hence, while it was relatively easy to abandon the idea of a subject's substantiality in social sciences, it implicitly persisted wherever its reflective categories assumed that substantiality. Descartes's philosophical discoveries hardly ever admit partial acceptance. Maybe this is where Gadamer's astonishment comes from when he ponders on the relation between theory and practice:

> What is it like, actually? Is theory ultimately practice, as already stressed by Aristotle, or is practice in general always at the same time theory, if it is only truly human practice? Is it not, being human, disregard for the self and looking at other people? Such life is a union of theory and practice, which every human being's opportunity and task. Overlooking the self, looking at what there is; it is a kind of educated, divine, so to speak, consciousness. It does not have to be a consciousness shaped by science and for science, but it has to be human educated consciousness, that has learnt to think others' points of view and seek communication regarding that what is common (*Gemeinsame*) and what is thought (*Gemeinte*).[64]

What drove a mind to seek consent between the common (*Gemeinsame*) and the thought (*Gemeinte*), lowered the prestige of the monadic *Cogito*

---

62 This is Habermas's concept of social sciences' task. Cf. Jürgen Habermas, *Pojęcie działania komunikacyjnego. (Uwagi wyjaśniające)*, (*The Notion of Communicational Activity (Explanatory Notes)*, trans. Andrzej M. Kaniowski, „Kultura i Społeczeństwo" 1986, no. 3, p. 21.

63 This is how the issue was construed in interactional symbolism.

64 Gadamer, *Pochwała teorii (Praise of Theory)*, pp. 37-38.

in the area of social sciences, as well as in philosophy itself. Gadamer, portraying the problem in historical categories, thoughti the first separation of theory from practice had already taken place in ancient philosophy. He sees this separation in the rise of theory as a new form of intellectual culture, which stood in revolutionary opposition to technology and practice, forms of knowledge and human activity conceptualised much earlier in the area of pre-philosophical thought, firmly rooted in Greek mentality. The social, open for everyone, communal character of these forms of knowledge and practice was beyond any doubt. Greek philosophers, in turn, who separated the domain of theory and gave it a special cognitive status, marked a definite boundary fencing it from practice. They attributed the "aristocratic" merit of selflessness to the former, while endowed the latter with a role in experiencing the self, which was supposed to take place in a social process and, consequently, subject to only limited intellectual control. Another axis of division assumed that intellectual activity had the potential to create a subjective self, whereas practices were seen as trivial and mechanical, possibly gravitating towards routine. Nevertheless, even these rather archaic dualisms did not tear pure knowledge (insight) apart from human existence. As Aristotle wrote: "Among thoughts those are free which can be chosen for themselves, whereas those which lead to knowledge concerning something else, are similar to slaves".[65]

How many forms of mental involvement can set a human being free? What does such a life strategy look like that shapes the *ethos* affirming the cognitive powers of mind? These questions refer not only to the relation between theory and practice, but also to the hierarchy of values allowing to assess thoughts in regard to their value in life and shape forms of living consistent with these assessments.

The first separation, depicted by Gadamer,[66] refers to the historic situation which Bourdieu links with the emergence of "scholastic mind" and

---

65 Aristotle, *Zachęta do filozofii (Protrepticus)*, trans. Kazimierz Leśniak, in: *Dzieła wszystkie (Collected Works)*, vol. 6, Wydawnictwo Naukowe PWN, Warszawa 2001, p. 640.

66 Hans-Georg Gadamer, *Theory, Technology, Praxis*, in: Hans-Georg Gadamer, *The Enigma of Health: The Art of Healing in a Scientific Age*, trans. James Gaiger and Nicholas Walker, Polity Press, Oxford 1996, pp. 4-5.

the "scholastic point of view", formed in special conditions: in time free from the toil of everyday chores (*schole*), away from the trouble of practical everyday life. It is in the conditions of the ancient *schole*, "free time", that the meaning of the primordial *theoria* underwent the first essential metamorphosis.[67] Since then theory has no longer been understood as it had been in pre-classical Greece: as a journey, a pilgrimage, accompanied by physical effort, the feeling of anxiety about the future, and even delight and deep experience of what is happening, and finally an intense experience of a self in the change anticipated by an oracle's utterance. In *schole* everything that had initially made up a *theoros*'s (envoy-pilgrim's) activity, becomes transformed into a distanced and systematic view, devoid of consequences for everyday life. It is indeed a form of disinvolvement, detachment, neutrality in relation to what is happening in the human world. At the same time all of it was stuck in the social world allowing the opposition of two lifestyles: *bios theoretikos* and *bios praktikos*. School in its diverse forms known in Western culture was to take over the *schole*. On the one hand, it has deprived theory of all the aspects where it comes up as activity and direct experience. On the other it retained the almost religious prestige attributed to the value which is truth, consequently securing theory the right to dominate over practice.[68]

However, the second separation of theory and practice, completed in the 17th century, is, according to Gadamer,[69] incomparably more significant for the present situation of sciences, thinking about theory and practice, for development prospects of social and human sciences. The development of natural sciences and their part in the gamut of applied inventions provoking social changes, has exerted pressure on human sciences. Namely, the latter have faced the requirement to meet criteria of

---

67 Cf. Pierre Bourdieu, *Pascalian Meditations*, trans. Richard Nice, Stanford Univ. Press, California 2000, p. 13.

68 Cf. Mariola Kuszyk-Bytniewska, *Dylemat rozumu scholastycznego: racjonalne kontra socjologiczne rekonstrukcje rozwoju wiedzy (Dilemma of a scholastic reason: rational versus sociological reconstructions of the delelopment knowledge)*, „Annales UMCS", sectio I, Philosophia-Sociologia, 2010, vol. XXXV, vol. 2, pp. 199-200.

69 Gadamer, *Pochwała teorii (Praise of Theory)*, p. 43.

scientificity formulated by scientism. In consequence, the subject of social and human sciences have been significantly narrowed by modern science and technology to fit in the boundaries marked by "application". Practice and technology have undergone a mutual reduction and subjugation to, at least *de iure*, application of theory. This way theory ceased to be an unbiased, selfless view, in favour of sciences' involvement in the world by means disciplined by a method. The view, the investigation, becomes embodied in an object and in technological, productive activity. Theory described this way keeps distance and disinvolvement only in relation to everyday *praxis*, seeking universal reference to reality outside experiences known from everyday life.

Probably nothing has changed its meaning more than this very notion of experience. On the one hand, its meaning has been limited to purely cognitive functions, cleansed of existential contexts, which was later, in the 19th century, to become an insurmountable problem for the nascent empirical human sciences. „Unlike natural sciences, though, all other sources of experience have a certain common characteristic. Their knowledge becomes an experience only when it gets included in the agent's practical activity."[70] This thought of Gadamer indicates how important existential aspects of experience are and perfectly captures the specific nature of human sciences – humanities and social sciences, in relation to natural sciences. In the latter, the exact opposite holds: experience acquires value for knowledge only when it gets purified of links to the agent's (*resp.* the experimenter's) practical consciousness.

On the other hand, the notion of experience, freed from practical contexts, could be almost unboundedly expanded by modern science, with the use of scientific technology. Experience could then step outside the tradition-infused everyday lifeworlds, bounded by human powerlessness and activity inefficiency.

So experience, as construed in modern times, has acquired a special meaning: it has been detached from any situation of an acting individual, from all links to action, both as an aspect of cognition and as its potential subject matter. Scientific experience has been separated from practical

---

70 Gadamer, *Theory, Technology, Praxis*, in: Gadamer, *The Enigma of Health*, p. 2.

experiences because it has been imposed with methodical and technical requirements, such as verifiability, availability, repeatability, possibility to determine results on a certain scale adopted beforehand. This way it has become research. The prestige of "experience" understood as the epistemic and moral *summum bonum* of prudent conduct, has rapidly inflated in an ever more fluid, critical to the past, lifeworld. As Gadamer says, we could see the limiting of all experience-based knowledge to scientific experience.[71] Since the 17th century, "only that which could be verified could have validity as experience",[72] hence only that which can be placed in an experiment.[73] Thus maybe this kind of experience should be more fittingly called "scientific experiment" or "scientific research" instead of plain "experience". By keeping the name of "experience" in modern natural sciences, we unwittingly reduce its former meaning to laboratory practices.

What is the area of life called practice then? What is its relation to theory, to science, and to human existence? Must practice, driven by changes triggered by modernity, mean only application of science? Gadamer hits the point, saying:

> For practice means not only the making of whatever one can make; it is also choice and decision between possibilities. Practice always has a relationship to a person's 'being'.[74]

Practice is a kind of connection between a human being and their life environment, thus it means a decision and a choice from an array of possibilities.

---

71 Cf. Gadamer, *Theory, Technology, Praxis*, in: Gadamer, *The Enigma of Health*, p. 3.

72 Gadamer, *Theory, Technology, Praxis*, in: Gadamer, *The Enigma of Health*, p. 5.

73 Of the modern narrowing of the notion of experience, cf. Hans-Georg. Gadamer, *Truth and Method*, second revised edition, trans. revised by Joel Weinsheimer and Donald G. Marshall, Continuum, London, New York 2006, pp. 341-355. Cf. also Mariola Kuszyk-Bytniewska, *Czy racjonalność jest „miejscem wspólnym" doświadczenia religijnego i naukowego? (Is Rationality a Common Place of Religious and Scientific Experience?)*, „Przegląd Religioznawczy" 2010, no. 4 (238), pp. 43-56.

74 Gadamer, *Theory, Technology, Praxis*, in: Gadamer, *The Enigma of Health*, pp. 3-4.

That practice is related to *phronesis*, to prudence, making choices, taking decisions, and finally to knowledge, which can be clearly seen in medical "practice", as the latter has retained much of its tradition and from its standpoint in relation to human beings and knowledge, but it also, as practice, functions under the pressure of technological achievements.[75] Not only in medical sciences, but above all in human and social sciences, sciences which study human beings, their creations, activities, thoughts, practice and theory cannot be separated, set in opposition. Theories of social activities are also governed by the practical mind, not just theoretical. They are involved, they shape social practices and must be aware of it.

In social sciences comprehension of this state of affairs has grown slowly and with resistance from positivism, naturalism and scientism, shaping these sciences' self-awareness since their beginnings. Only in the 20th century did the so-called anti-positivist breakthrough, in social sciences present for example in the work of Znaniecki, change the theoretical situation. That work has been more recently continued by Bourdieu, Elias, Giddens, and especially Taylor.

---

75 This was pointed out by Gadamer, but also Zbigniew Szawarski, who indirectly asks, in his book *Mądrość i sztuka leczenia* (*Wisdom and the Art of Healing*), the following questions: who do you have to be in order to be a good doctor? Is medicine a science, an art or a practice? What does the art of treatment depend on? The art. Of treatment is, he says, "a certain system of medical activities and practices aiming at healing the patient". Technology and practice are connected in application (this is how it has been since the the beginning of modernity, hence the confusion of notions) and this is why Szawarski writes that a doctor's practice is mainly *techne* and he sees it in opposition to *episteme*. A good doctor is a wise doctor, a doctor having knowledge (not only medical knowledge, but also that about the world and of people; not only knowledge of facts, but also of their meaning), good judgement ("an ability to apply general and abstract knowledge or rules in particular situations"), as well as self-confidence, confidence in his/her thoughts, choices (actions) and convictions. Cf. Zbigniew Szawarski, *Mądrość i sztuka leczenia (Wisdom and the Art of Healing)*, Wydawnictwo słowo/obraz terytoria, Gdańsk 2006, p. 383. See also Hans-Georg Gadamer, *Apologia for the Art of Healing*, in: Gadamer, *The Enigma of Health: The Art of Healing in a Scientific Age*, pp. 31-44 and Gadamer, *Theory, Technology, Praxis*, in: Gadamer, *The Enigma of Health*, pp. 19-22.

Chapter II Onto-Epistemological Transgression of Epistemocentrism

Onto-epistemology means relinquishing the area of research and reflection appropriated by epistemocentric philosophy to social sciences. This appropriation was carried out in absence of human and social sciences in the modern knowledge order. Their rise has changed the situation, though. Epistemocentric philosophy has shaped these sciences' self-awareness in a possessive manner, absorbing the experience of social life into its own paradigms and deforming them in the spirit of *schole*. Epistemocentric philosophy had already settled what a "subject" is, what "knowledge" is, as well as "experience" or "the world". At the same time, the nascent sociology was refused to propose its own definitions, using the privilege determined by epistemocentrism. Refusal to acknowledge scientific competences of social sciences, which were to be censored by epistemology – not as much the queen as the supervisor of sciences – or laborious efforts to fit them into the methodological framework of natural sciences, belong to history now. Still, the trouble with acknowledging their scientificity has remained. Questions about their autonomy in relation to other disciplines, and even their purpose, continue to be asked. Since they are asked with regard to their relative position to study of nature, they are still valid wherever the idea of methodological unity of all scientific knowledge is treated seriously.

Nowadays social sciences and humanities are perceived as quite autonomous from their social and cultural environment, which allows them to create their own disciplinary traditions. They are professionalised to the extent that guarantees them inclusion in the contemporary knowledge order. Nevertheless, they do not share the models of scientific activity elaborated by scientism. That is why almost since their very beginnings a strong conviction has formed of the need to apply a broader conceptual apparatus, more capable of differentiating scientific knowledge than it used to be in the 20th-century philosophy of science. These concepts appealing to humanists include for example Foucault's notion of *episteme*

or "discourse". We can also, following Hans Lenk, adopt a "relatively lib-
eral understanding of science": „»an idea of science balancing« between
extreme postulates and concepts accepting diversity of assumptions and
description forms forged in the process of social sciences' development
to date".[76] In this context, Gadamer's critique of methodologism is note-
worthy, too. This state of affairs is definitely affected by the awareness of
growing diversity in intellectual and social roles played by sciences in the
modern world. Modernity imposed on us the idea of universal and homo-
geneous science, with no respect to the diversity of subject matter, purposes,
methods, disciplinary traditions, cognitive and extra-cognitive functions
of knowledge. At present, in the face of various forms of knowledge's influence on social realities, the following question gains importance: what
determines whether a particular discourse or creation of thought becomes
a science? How can it enter the order of knowledge attained by existing
sciences? What is its specific disciplinary tradition? What relations link it
with its cultural environment? Only later, for completely different reasons,
a question may arise why certain "thought collectives" (e.g. the thought
collective oriented at epistemology) accept, and others do not accept its
claims to being a scientific discourse.

1. Arbitrary and ideological orders of science: A consequence of the unitary model of knowledge

The difference between humanistic and naturalistic investigation was already demonstrated in the 19th and early 20th centuries by such thinkers
as Wilhelm Dilthey, Heinrich Rickert, Max Weber, Wilhelm Windelband,
Ernst Cassirer, and Florian Znaniecki. It was seen in the specific subject
matter (culture vs nature, society vs nature, spirit vs psyche) or in the
method (interpretation vs explanation, description vs law). In my perception, though, the errors in thinking about sociology and other social sciences or humanities as sciences lay in seeing them as derivative cognitive

---

76 Hans Lenk, *Filozofia pragmatycznego interpretacjonizmu. Filozofia między
nauką a praktyką. (Philosophy of Pragmatic Interpretationism. Philosophy between Science and Practice)*, trans. Zbigniew Zwoliński, Oficyna Wydawnicza
Naukowa, Warszawa 1995, p. 146.

phenomena in relation to methodologically privileged sciences: physics, mathematics, as well as biology or economics. The division of humanities into "hard" and "soft" disciplines seems to maintain this reductionism.

In turn, the specific character of humanities as opposed to social sciences manifests largely in the fact that the former analyse, describe and interpret phenomena so as to convey their individual traits, even when they are located in the context of the anonymous social, semiotic or psychological sphere. Meanwhile, social sciences seem to follow the opposite direction, describing rules involving sets of (social, semiotic, psychological etc.) phenomena, transferring knowledge of them to the sphere of their individual understanding.

Further on, I am going to use the notion of "social sciences", not "humanities". My choice is informed by the observation that social sciences, provided the anti-scientistic interpretation, are also humanistic in the meaning given, for example, by the idea of the "humanistic coefficient".[77] So construed social sciences, including also sociology, I treat as a non-scientistic (understood in a non-positivist spirit) area of research, endowed with the potential to turn into science (in the meaning of a methodically and socially bounded discourse, with a purpose, methods, object of study, institutional and professional regime). I mean a science examining relations between structures and dynamics of groups of people and images of reality and behaviours shaped by them. These links cannot be captured either by investigating only society (as a subject of positivist sociology) or by investigating only individuals (e.g. in the light of psychology or existential philosophy). Social sciences are sciences acknowledging indispensability of the onto-epistemological moment in social thought. This means that their components are not only theories and their technological extensions, but also practices, hardly available for the conceptual apparatus formed in the early modern (epistemocentrically narrowed) manner of scientific study.

Among social sciences sociology will be my main area of exploration, especially as construed by Znaniecki, distinguished from culture sciences

---

77 Cf. Florian Znaniecki, *The Method of Sociology*, Rinehart & Company, Inc. New York 1934, pp. 36-39.

and the closest to philosophy, a model for others.[78] Therefore I roam the area that could be described, for focus and clarity of reasoning, as onto-epistemologically oriented philosophy of sociology. Sociology is a science particularly destined to adopt the ideas of onto-epistemology, both due to its history, related to the emergence of a new, institutionally reflective society, and due to its specific link to its subject. The scientific character of sociology must, therefore, be understood specifically: it lies in sociology's onto-epistemological autonomy, attained not by separation from other sciences, but by onto-epistemological emancipation executed by means of philosophy. The onto-epistemological moment reveals here in the forms of social being proper to modernity, where knowledge becomes an important actor of social life. Social reality formed by modernity assumes indispensable participation of science in social practices. Without that participation, neither social science nor social practices would have a distinctively modern shape. Thus we encounter strong bonds linking methods and cognitive strategies of social sciences with motivations and subjects of study entangled in modern forms of social practices. These bonds have been overlooked by the 19th-century idea of Science created by scientism. That idea imposed homogeneity of language, methods, principles, and even content, on valuable knowledge. Nevertheless, the concept of science is ambiguous: for its historic metamorphoses, its multiple disciplines, for the ever-growing body of knowledge and ever-changing participation of science in social reality. This participation is nowadays approved of, not only for the spirit of innovation inscribed in science, but also for the confirmed efficiency of its technological applications.

Since early modernity, elaborated ideals of knowledge have repeatedly left social sciences outside the margin of acceptable departure from science. Those areas of knowledge which dealt with social reality, culture, human actions, eluded the perspective of sciences like physics or later biology, that have achieved cognitive and technological success and have become a steady support for the prestige of knowledge in the modern era.

---

78 Cf. Florian Znaniecki, *Cultural Sciences. Their Origin and Development*, University of Illinois Press, Urbana 1952, Preface & chap. XIV; Florian Znaniecki, *Social Relation and Social Roles. The Unfinished Systematic Sociology*, Chandler Publishing Company, San Francisco 1965, pp. 3-20.

The paradox in this state of affairs is as follows: on the one hand, scientific knowledge is very highly regarded in the modern order of values reigning in the human world; on the other hand, when it comes to social self-examination constituting a scientific discipline (i.e. sociology), it is over and over questioned and its statements debatable.

The causes of the constant discrepancy between the ideal of knowledge and the real scopes of scientific disciplines in modern culture should be identified in the 19th century intellectual climate, nursing the belief in science's uniformity, based on highly restrictive philosophical postulates. The legacy of Newton and Descartes incessantly nurtured the conviction that one is the world and one should be the science of it. *Sapientia universalis* was meant to embrace all knowledge, including all philosophy to date. In this vein, physics was elected queen by scholars. Therefore social sciences, born only in the second half of the 19th century, found a ready ideal of science, forged in the intellectual experience of natural sciences, and did not have the opportunity to forge their own. Hence they were compelled to accept the intellectual dominance of natural sciences and make concessions to that ideal, which involved declaring empiricism and observance of the rigours of nomothetic science, also in areas where profitability of such an approach was not at all obvious. I mean, above all, the 19th-century scientistic thinking of newly appeared human sciences. This arbitrary decision, whose principal goal was to introduce humanists to the world of "true" science, relegated considerations of the broadly understood human sciences, in the spirit of *artes*, to the outskirts of knowledge. This led to discrimination of "different rationalities", which eluded the scientistic mind. Questions about motives, objectives, ways of experiencing a human being's identity and emotional bonds between an individual and a group which he or she belongs to along with the Other, whom he or she meets: all of that had to be abandoned on the grounds of science, since in science the set of four forms of causality distinguished by Aristotle shrank to just one, agency.

The problem of what is scientific, or, in other words, of social sciences' theoretical autonomy, is as old as the world where these sciences came into being, and discussed as much as social reality to which they refer. Their debatable status has been expressed since they appeared and all the time during their formation. No wonder. On the one hand, social sciences themselves took up the difficult, often controversial function of expressing the consciousness of the modern era. The ideal of science they encountered, accepted or rejected, became an obstacle for acknowledgement of what was now seen as knowledge's equally precious values: its methodological unity and technological efficiency. On the other hand, modernity, still *in statu nascendi*, as still unfinished and not fully defined, has endlessly allocated new places for these sciences in social projects brought into being. They were meant to shape, sanction, design or assess social realities, which were seen as possible to embrace rationally, both in the practical meaning and the intellectual one. The roles of commenting modernity, and at the same time, participant of changes in its inside, clashed every now and then, impeding understanding of these sciences' theoretical autonomy. That is why divisions (classifications, typologies) of sciences including social sciences usually were, and still are, largely arbitrary, as fruit of philosophical projects of valuable knowledge, however motivated by current assessment of modernity's progress. These divisions were and are as historically changeable as these very sciences. The history of pre-modern science documents debates and conflicts between scientific institutions, universities (like the Oxford – Paris debate in the Middle Ages), popes and kings against schools, between scholars and political systems etc. All these controversies influenced participation of a specific scientific theory, or science in general, in social life. That was true especially in case of all reflection on society. As remarked by Andrzej Bronk and Stanisław Majdański, "in case of »the human world« (*Lebenswelt*), which includes science, order is a human accomplishment", "people not only bring culture to life, but also give it an intentional order", and "in the world of culture ordering depends not as much on discovering independently existing, »natural« order, as on its arbitrary construction".[79] However, this "arbitrary construction" of orders in sciences dealing with social world and the world of culture cannot be permanently established, nor is it independent from social practices.

---

79 Andrzej Bronk, Stanisław Majdański, *Kłopoty z przyporządkowaniem nauk: perspektywa naukoznawcza (The Dilemma with Cognitive Categorization of Scientific Disciplines. A Methodological Point of View)*, „Nauka" 2009, no. 1, p. 50.

Such a situation, when only intellectual factors are taken into account, results also from philosophy's "blindness" of sorts, which, facing modern science's claims cannot cope with reference to processes shaping it and shaping its orders. The difficulty in philosophy's location in relation to sciences and its alleged "blindness" was adequately described by Siemek in the article *"Nauka" i "naukowość" jako ideologiczne kategorie filozofii* (*"Science" and "Scientific" as Ideological Categories of Philosophy*).[80] He says that until the time when modern science came into being the notions of philosophy and science had been considered the same thing. The particular and general character of knowledge, essential insight and empirical investigation, intuition and formality did not stand in radical opposition, at least not to the extent allowing to draw the "philosophy – science" division. It is interesting that since modern scientific discourse came up, little has changed in this relation. Philosophy still refers to science as if it was a science too and only the 19th century brought radical change: philosophy, identifying itself with new science, carried out a self-reduction, and consequently, destruction of its basic, classical conceptualisations.[81] Then philosophy in the form of an ideology called scientism strove to create conditions, categories and concepts of scientific description of reality, transforming into a metascience, *de facto* not as much "science about science", as a dogmatic, epistemocentric programme. Anti-metaphysical philosophies, formed in those times, essentially introduced epistemocentric assumptions of science and eliminated all debatable philosophical questions concerning the status of social sciences. The rejected concepts of social environment and, above all, action and its practical organisation, cumulate in a loftily humanistic (and defying scientism), though unscientific, programme, in the shape of philosophy of living.

By scientism Siemek understands *"philosophy* that sees science as an entity separate from it and therefore as an object of questions. This way it discredits the old, philosophical concept of »science« (based on the very *lack* of such a distinction) and at the same time strives to remove this

---

80 Cf. Marek J. Siemek, *"Nauka" i "naukowość" jako ideologiczne kategorie filozofii* (*"Science" and "Scientism" as Ideological Categories of Philosophy*), "Studia Filozoficzne" 1983, no. 5-6, pp. 71-84.
81 Cf. Siemek, p. 75.

distinction in its theoretical self-awareness, hence, defend this old concept".[82] Scientism is an approach born inside philosophy and is strictly philosophical. It states that only scientific research provides valuable knowledge. Simultaneously, by issuing statements about values, it becomes a philosophical stance which attempts to carefully conceal it using a structure of logically disciplined discourse on science and the scientific, its criteria, language, methods etc.

Therefore, the words "science" and "scientific" seen in this perspective are concepts that express deluded hopes of philosophy itself: they are tools of philosophy's false self-consciousness in reference to the reality of cognition and knowledge, because they allow to keep the privilege to norm and codify all knowledge on the grounds of not philosophy's own, but alien (none other than scientific!) intellectual experiences. Scientistic notions create a false image of science for purely philosophical needs, that is "for internal use" in philosophical debates, which can (and often must) erroneously settle many problems of science.[83] And this state of affairs does not change in the face of rising empirical sciences on human beings and their culture: sociology, psychology, cultural anthropology. They do not provoke, by their very existence, any particular corrections of this stance. All these areas of humanistic and social study, Siemek argues, surrender to the repressive ideology and accept the ideological order of science elaborated by scientism and strengthened by positivism. Not only the concepts of what is science and what is scientific are ideological, but also other notions lying at their sources and taking part in describing and assessing knowledge, such as rationality, objectivity, experience, subject, knowledge. They are constructed to meet the needs of philosophy seeing itself as a scientific of meta-scientific discourse.

---

82 Cf. Siemek, p. 76.

83 For example, due to this ideology, neo-positivism excluded from physics (even) Newtonian principles, because they do not meet the scientific criteria. It is because the formula: "all bodies gravitate to one another" cannot be subject to empirical verification. Instead, scientific status is granted to the statement: "each of the objects examined so far in mechanics falls onto the ground". This requirement makes, in turn, "laws of nature" and even "laws of science". There is no greater harm to theory than invalidating the category of "law" as a universal category, as well as integrating knowledge.

This issue is similarly addressed by Gadamer:

Philosophy itself became a problematic enterprise. What sort of philosophy is still possible alongside the sciences, after the development of modern natural science and its encyclopedic treatment in the seventeenth and eighteenth centuries, is the question all modern philosophy faces.[84]

August Comte, Herbert Spencer, Émile Durkheim, Max Weber – all of them, not without significant differences between their theories, want to create scientific sociology. And although all of them, especially the latter two, deeply understand the specific character of sociology's subject, they surrender their theories to the scientific imperative to the extent of constructing an empiricist strategy which proves that their scientific programmes can be accepted in the spirit of scientism. Durkheim adopts this stance in the form of a methodological principle ("study social facts as things"), while Weber embraces it in the postulate of "value-free sociology". To study social facts as things means here not to take into account the social fact of science, and to postulate sociology free from judgement means to postulate the value of social science as a purely epistemological qualification independent of modern reality.

The conclusion from the above considerations is as follows: since natural and humanistic sciences differ substantially in their subjects, their ability to involve extra-cognitive actions, the ability to profit from experiencing them, hence also manners of description, then there is no unique, philosophically justified or scientifically well-grounded, order of sciences. Sciences apply different methodologies, driven by various goals and motives to acquire knowledge, and the roles that the results of studious efforts play in the social world differ too. Therefore there are multiple orders ruling cognition, because they have socially, historically and epistemologically diverse functions, not always congruous with one another. Their (technological or practical) relations to social reality are also diverse. Thus typologies or classifications of sciences are not objective in the meaning of reflecting a certain order or orders existing before their onset. Neither do they mirror any archetypical order of knowledge to which sciences converge following ultimate epistemological or metaphysical verdicts. These

84 *Hans-Georg Gadamer on Education, Poetry, and History*, p. 212.

classifications are not even true to the historic, contingent order of knowledge. Constructions of this kind are rather built to meet certain needs and
with respect to purposes resident most often within philosophy and its current programme, put together under the pressure of philosophical debate.

Orders of scientific knowledge constructed from a theoretical meta-
reference are also arbitrary. They are results of philosophical projects and
convictions concerning the history of science, understanding the tasks of
epistemology etc., rather than results of reasonings recommended by scientism, that is, in the area of empirical research in the history of scientific
study's products. This does not mean that these orders are not supported
by any rationale. Disciplines of knowledge differ from one another according to many criteria. Hence the open space to introduce distinctions
where, inevitably, natural genres of science do not exist.

The awareness of this state of affairs (including plural views on what
is scientific, unlike in the tradition of research in natural sciences) shapes
debates in the area of social sciences, concerning relations between science
and social realities. The principal ideas, crucial for onto-epistemological
approach to these issues, are born in sociology. Ossowski, Znaniecki,
Bourdieu (and not only them) perfectly knew about it.

2. Sociology as a special representative of social sciences

None of modern sciences has been subject to so many so controversial
entrance exams to the world of science as sociology. Methodological sus-
picion is roused by its relatively young age, not fitting into the disciplinary
order formed by sciences *par excellence*, penchant for multiple paradigms,
and finally to ideological bias or banality (triviality) of uttered statements.
Sociology has had to face objections of this kind since the very beginning.
It has had to defend its conceptualisations of social reality and prove that
they are rational and critical. It could do so only as an autonomous scientific discipline.

The departure point of sociological research, and at the same time a
substitute for experiment, is observation of social reality from the perspective of a participant. However, the misleading demon present in this
observation, described by Descartes, can dominate in sociological investigation not only because the investigating mind, due to its finiteness, is

prone to illusion. It is rather because this demon acts (misleads) through the object of observation and there it reveals its presence. Note that modernity as a cultural formation manifests, among others, in expanding of social reality by symbolic products of human creativity. This results in reality adopting elements of fiction (virtual worlds, participation of social prognoses in reality, mass media etc.), that is, severance of signs from real things marked by them. Signs, thus, acquire an independent role of objects and instruments of activity, of a highly indeterminate use. That is why sociology as a critical science not so much unveils reality in accordance with the Cartesian-Kantian paradigm, as analyses the creative role of the aforementioned fiction, its participation in social life. Hence modern sociology is also a reflective science. This means that sociology is equipped with forms of cognition capturing social changes, while being capable of assessing its ontic participation in reality. For sociology itself belongs to the domain of results obtained by the symbolic activity of modern people and has its place among other creations of spiritual culture. Sociology affects reality and reflects on it at the same time. It affects the process of adopting fiction into social life, as it makes its own reflective influence part of social agents' practices. In consequence it must detach itself from its own sources, which poses a difficult test of its maturity. Difficult, because it always entails questioning tradition-sanctioned, model (paradigmatic) achievements referring to reality that does not exist anymore.

This is appropriately illustrated by Wittgenstein's ladder metaphor:

> My propositions serve as elucidations in the following way: anyone who understands me eventually recognizes them as nonsensical, when he has used them – as steps – to climb up beyond them. (He must, so to speak, throw away the ladder after he has climbed up it.)
> He must transcend these propositions, and then he will see the world aright.[85]
> Sociology as a science about action could appear only in modernity, mature enough to reflectively "leave the epistemological ladder behind", to reassess the value of common sense and reason for the sociological theory. Early modernity abandoned the tradition of practical philosophy, known since Aristotle. It entrusted Descartes, bringing the idea of the theoretical mind's autonomy into life and restricting "common sense" to areas that refuse to be ordered according

85 Ludwig Wittgenstein, *Tractatus logico-philosophicus*, Routledge, London-New York 2002, p. 89.

to categories of the scientific mind. That "common sense" came to be treated as a set of recommendations of thinking and acting in the "experienced world" (*Lebenswelt*), always remaining a mere object of theory. No wonder, as only in the modern era did the Reason of Copernicus, Descartes and Newton question certainty as the value of direct, local and personal experience, which is spontaneously shaped by common sense. When the theoretical mind triumphed over what is experienced in action, a path for sociology opened, neglecting the cognitive scruples of common sense and practical philosophy. Now sociology was able to determine its cognitive task as a drive towards certainty guaranteed by theory and aiming at the future.

This relation of sociology to sciences and, more widely, to intellectual culture, became possible thanks to changes brought by modernity. As a result, modernity as a cultural formation remains in a theoretically privileged relation to the area of reality that Aristotle had described as the space of "what is capable of being otherwise". Modernity paves the way for social theory. Contrary to Aristotle, in modernity this space is construed as historically ordered, which definitely collides with his understanding of both conditions of practical activity that can be undertaken in this area and his understanding of the relation between theory and practice. Modernity clears the path for theory (representation) in relation to the reality of action.

> It is to be noted that nothing that is past is an object of choice, e.g. no one chooses to
> have sacked Troy; for no one *deliberates* about the past, but about what is future and capable of being otherwise, while what is past is not capable of not having taken place; hence Agathon is right in saying:
> For this alone is lacking even to god,
> To make undone things that have once been done.[86]

The past, says Aristotle, is irreversible and as such, remains outside the area of what is "capable of being otherwise". Therefore it does not determine the principles and norms of human activity, principles and norms of practice. Those reside in human nature and they cannot be intellectually extricated from the contingency of human behaviours. For Aristotle, the historical dimension of action, paradoxical as it sounds, simply does not

---

86 Aristotle, *The Nicomachean Ethics*, p. 104.

exist.[87] Moreover, activity cannot be an object of objective representation: as practice, it connects to intellect through deliberation and decision, as opposed to distanced observation. Therefore the fact that the past cannot be an object of action, does not mean that it enters the domain of "what is not capable of being otherwise", that it becomes a plausible object of contemplation and representation, hence, theory. The past is merely an object of certain narrations, histories, but not practice or theory. The passing of things frees human activity both from the past and from theoretical considerations, it opens the field for deliberation.

In modern thinking about the past and forms of modern practices, we have to do with utterly different relations. We can be free from the past not thanks to the passing of everything, but thanks to the reflective mind, which steps outside the current situation, showing the past as a closed chapter. It is possible because from the modern intellectual perspective history is metamorphoses of the very social reality, not merely someone's tale. The past, as each time, has its normed form. Passing, as a property of actions, is seen here as the presence of the past and the future in the current moment, the presence significantly affecting possibilities of action. This is because action is bounded not only by human nature. It is also bounded by the contingent character of principles ruling the life environment forged in the past, an environment that suppresses nature and brings imperfection into the world (as seen by Rousseau). Hence reflection has a critical character and inevitably refers to the future: the time of critical trial for the present and also the time of change. Similarly, the function of intellect in relation to action manifests in a different way than the Stagirite's practical philosophy predicts. The role of intellect is giving way to action driven by reflection informed by theory. Reflection shows contingency of the

---

87 Aristotle still did not know the concept of historical thinking, the idea of history as a teacher of life (*historia magistra vitae*), nor did he accept the Pythagorean principle of its eternal return. Modernity likewise rejects the latter idea, but it links historicity with the idea of progress, unknown to Aristotle. Cf. on this Reinhart Koselleck, *Historia Magistra Vitae: The Dissolution of the Topos into the Perspective of a Modernized Historical Process*, in: Reinhart Koselleck, *Futures Past on the Semantics of Historical Time*, Columbia Univ. Press, New York 2004, pp. 26-42.

passing reality's conditions only when it is capable of showing directions of emancipation from the limits of what is passing. The change of action conditions can only come with reflection, a source of distance to the current events and of the need for critique and innovation.

Thus, modernity gives rise to a completely new opportunity for thinking: the possibility to relate theory to the future. Openness to the future lay at the foundation of modern optimism, expressed in the belief in the ability to shape the future (also the individual future, within the doctrine). The idea of "progress" (and later "development", too) relegated tradition to the role of a burden, a superstition blocking free design of social life. As a utopia, the modern critique of the contingent past is a creation of reflection and defiance of tradition, a fossil of common sense and routine experience. Sociology, however, steps beyond the pattern of utopia thanks to a possibility that practical philosophy had not known and had not predicted. The future as seen in a pre-modern way could not be subject to theory, but only to the practical mind. It is only modernity that made a reflective view of the past possible, and the model of a natural science, whose main value came to be predicting effects, proved extraordinarily inspiring.

In that matter, two questions are worth mentioning:

First, sociology chooses actions as its primary object of research: a combination of behaviours shaped by and shaping social actors and their environment, along with what refers to the future. The future can be influenced and remains in a fluent bond with the past, already complete and petrified in effects and works, only subject to interpretations and judgements, the knowledge of it can be disseminated or ignored. This obviously does not remove the possibility to shape reference to the past and interpretation of tradition, although depending on how the future is designed. Rationalisation of history as products of early modernity's intellectual culture has forged a situation in which "the future" is capable of a specific, historical reassumption of "the past" using mainly discursive means of its fictionalisation. This engenders a risk of destruction to the body of collective experience, as remarked scrupulously by Gadamer. On the other hand, this risk is taken by modern culture often and with eagerness, attaching special value to its own means of reflection. Foucault says:

As to the problem of fiction, it seems to me to be a very important one; I am well aware that I have never written anything but fictions. I do not mean to say, however, that truth is therefore absent. It seems to me that the possibility exists for fiction to function in truth, for a fictional discourse to induce effects of truth, and for bringing it about that a true discourse engenders or "manufactures' something that does not as yet exist, that is, 'fictions' it. One 'fictions' history on the basis of a political reality that makes it true, one 'fictions' a politics not yet in existence on the basis of a historical truth.[88]

It is thanks to Foucault's "fictioning" that actuality spans the past and the future. And made real this way, they become objects of action.

Second, normativity and involvement are specific traits of sociological discourse. It refers not to what is and what was, but to what is in the context of what can be or should be. Therefore an attempt to do laboratory sociology (sterilised of values and meanings) is bound to fail.

Thus, sociology appears as a specific scientific discourse, conceptualising modern, reflective, fast-changing society, whose social order assumes products of intellectual culture participating in it, including sociology itself.

3. Epistemocentrism: An epistemological obstacle and the source of recurrent crises of social theories

In the context of portraying problems of "scholastic epistemocentrism", Bourdieu quotes the words of Bachelard, who created the concept of an "epistemological obstacle"[89]: "the world in which one thinks is not the world in which one lives."[90] Bachelard thought that common sense and science are completely different intellectual "worlds" ("fields" in Bourdieu's terms[91]), hence there is no continuity between knowledge informed by common sense and scientific knowledge. In the development of

---

88 Michel Foucault, *The History of Sexuality*, in: Michel Foucault, *Power/Knowledge. Selected Interviews and other Writings 1972-1977,* Pantheon Books, New York 1980, p. 193.

89 Cf. Gaston Bachelard, *The Formation of the Scientific Mind. A Contribution to a Psychoanalysis of Objective Knowledge,* introduced, trans. and ann. by Mary McAllester Jones, Clinamen Press, Manchester 2002, pp. 24-32.

90 Cf. e. g. Bourdieu, *Pascalian Meditations*, p. 51.

91 "In analytical categories field may be defined as a network or configuration of objective relations between positions." (Pierre Bourdieu and Loic J.D. Wacquant, *An Invitation to Reflexive Sociology*, p. 78). Fields are the various areas of human activity characterised by specific regulations. Cf. e. g. Patricia Thomson, *Field*, in: *Pierre Bourdieu: Key Concepts*, ed. Michael Grenfell, Acumen Publishing Limited, Durham 2010, pp. 67-81.

science, in order to pass from a notion to science, an epistemological leap (rupture) must occur. The history of science teaches us, says Bachelard, that it is a history of severances, errors, and discontinuous epistemological structures.

Although Bourdieu agrees with Bachelard[92] that severance is a necessary condition of science's development, he also thinks that the theoretical mind, projecting its understanding of the world on the practical mind, provokes complications and distortions of cognition. This "scholastic ethnocentrism" of sorts "leads [...] to cancelling out the specificity of practical logic". What we do have to do here with is „two socially constructed modes of construction and comprehension of the world": the scholastic one (constructed by scholars) and the practical one (created by people investigated by scholars).[93]

Bourdieu consciously refers to Pascal, representing a human point of view, and rejects Descartes's stance, representing a scholastic point of view contaminated with epistemocentrism. He admits that he owes his care for ordinary people to Pascal, as well as the healthy common sense and investigating causes of human behaviours, including those most preposterous and most inconsistent. Philosophy has „excessive confidence in the powers of language", thus above all we have "to reflect not only on the limits of thought and of the powers of thought, but also on the conditions in which it is exercised").[94]

Limited and specific participation of scholars in social practices, the "thinking style" developed by them, is transmitted epistemocentrically to the whole reality, making it a universal vision, an intellectual tool to capture all sorts of phenomena. Ludwik Fleck's notion of scholars' "*thought style*"[95] is, in Bourdieu's terms, the intellectual effect of the "scholastic point of view", elaborated in the conditions of suspended everyday

---

92 Bourdieu, in his conversation with Wacquant, frequently quotes Bachelard, among others the statement that in science the common-sense vision of the world needs to be abandoned.

93 Bourdieu, *Pascalian Meditations*, p. 51.

94 Bourdieu, *Pascalian Meditations*, p. 2.

95 Cf. Ludwik Fleck, *Genesis and Development of a Scientific Fact*, University of Chicago Press, 1981.

practices, practices of ordinary life. Independent view, exercised from a distance, intermediated with theory, thus becomes an obstacle to acquiring knowledge. Imposition of such a point of view (a particular one, as rooted in the position of a person of thought) on all knowledge, stands in the way of study where it is entangled in other practical forms of intelligibility). "This typically scholastic representation is based, as ever, on the substitution of a reflexive vision for the practical vision."[96]

The scholastic point of view, itself cut off from social life, establishes the norms of its own discourse, and this is the essence of epistemocentrism's intellectual self-confinement. Its history goes back to the beginnings of Western philosophy and already there it assumed the form of "scholastic disposition". It is because the genesis of scholastic mind is related to *skholè*: as explained by Bourdieu, with time free from chores, from practical cares, with the state of inaction.[97] *Skholèn agein* means to remain inert, savour peace, do nothing. At the same time *skholè* is a school that organises time free from practical chores, devoted to study. Science, (Western) philosophy, rose then in institutionalised conditions of thought liberated from the broad context of its participation in social reality, free from practical purposes. Of course, it is a milestone in the development of philosophy, or even a condition of its existence. This seems now an unproblematic statement, but it also causes limitations in investigating human activities, when it turns out that thought and cognition are present there in a different way than in pure thinking and cognition. Bourdieu says:

> The upshot of this is not that theoretic knowledge is worth nothing but that we must know its limits and accompany all scientific accounts with an account of the limits and limitations of scientific accounts: theoretical knowledge owes a number of its most essential properties to the fact that the conditions under which it is produced are not that of practice.[98]

"School" conditions shaped not only the freedom, the lightness of thought, but also a cult of sorts of the value of knowledge and a certain concept of being a subject, subjugated to the ideal of knowledge, as opposed to

---

96 Bourdieu, *Pascalian Meditations*, p. 207.
97 Cf. Bourdieu, *Pascalian Meditations*, p. 13.
98 Bourdieu, Wacquant, *An Invitation to Reflexive Sociology*, p. 70.

practices surrounding it. The scholastic point of view is based on and formed by social means, school as an institution, a neutralising disposition, in the sense similar to Husserl's *epoche*, implying the bracketing of all theses of existence and all practical intentions.[99] It idealises, that is, cuts off people and things from their context, while stressing the cognitive significance of such values as rationality, objectivity, intersubjectivity, detaching them from *praxis*. This disposition suspends convictions of common sense concerning the world and practical purposes of thinking. Since early modernity, when this disposition was developed within the metaphysics of *ego cogito*, adopting the scholastic point of view has been a tacitly assumed "permission card" required by all scientific fields. In other words, it is a kind of competence or a condition of doing science by any scholar: a naturalist or a humanist. The scientific, scholastic mind must be sterile and it must be constructed to scrupulously separate the world of thought from lifeworld, cognition from action: it is a condition of acknowledgement in the field of science.

This way, epistemocentrism, rooted in the ancient world, but especially characteristic to early modern philosophy, surfaced as an epistemological obstacle and a source of chronic crises of sociological theories. Epistemocentrism is an epistemological obstacle because the dominance of epistemology and the value of knowledge in philosophy and sciences, along with the epistemological fundamentalism and representationism, which enhance it, pose an obstacle for the growth of knowledge in social sciences. Those conceptualise practices and the presence of thought in them in a manner different from what is known to the scholastic mind. The Cartesian illusion of gaining an absolute, privileged perspective or a neutral point of view, is an obstacle in the way of humanist mind, an obstacle in acquiring a human being's self-awareness. Epistemocentrism makes understanding human behaviours more difficult by projecting its structure, objectives and means on these behaviours. It blocks understanding how knowledge takes part in social reality.

---

99 Cf. Pierre Bourdieu, *Practical Reason: On the Theory of Action*, Stanford Univ. Press, California 1998, p. 128.

Successes and popularity of epistemocentrism were contributed to by
the conceptual change that modernity has introduced to the dictionary of
Western intellectual culture. It depends on identifying practice (*praxis*) and
technology-art (*technè*), while assuming that the link between thought and
practice-technology depends on application, which results in objectification. The problem lies in the fact that in practice application is a utopia of
action order, whereas in technology it is reality. Intellectual projections of
this idea, utopias and dystopias, indirectly reveal early modern pretences
of the technological mind. Orwell's *1984* is a bitter irony-laden portrayal
of a world where, to slightly simplify things, the social world is meant to
function as an "application" of a theory. The imminent practical corrup-
tion of the idea in its application reveals the technological mind's dan-
gerous naïveté, which stems from lack of understanding that *praxis* is not
the same as *techné*, that the success of thought in its technological objectification does not have to, or maybe even cannot, be repeated in the field
of action. The notion of practice which includes both *techné*, production
activity, and activity within Aristotelian *praxis*, is an epistemological obstacle of a concept that has not been sufficiently analysed. The most important element of this obstacle for social sciences is the way of understanding
participation of thought in "practice-technology": as application of investigation results, investigation that has been efficiently exercised somewhere else, beyond practice, in the scholastically organised conditions of
thinking.

Epistemocentrism is, thus, a specific intellectual skew, a specific *epoche*
distorting the object of social study, it is reduction of practical reason to
applying theoretical reason, an outcome of "scholars' ethnocentrism".[100]
Bourdieu says:

> Like reason, which, according to Kant, tends to situate the principle of its
> judgements not in itself but in the nature of its objects, *scholastic epistemocentrism*
> engenders a totally unrealistic (and idealist) anthropology. Imputing to its object
> what belongs in fact to the way of looking at it, it projects into practice (with,
> for example, rational action theory) an unexamined social relation which is none
> other than the scholastic relation to the world. Taking various forms depending on
> the traditions and the domains of analysis, it places a meta-discourse (a grammar,

---

100 Cf. Pierre Bourdieu, *Homo Academicus*, Les Éditions de Minuit, Paris 1984.

a typical product of the scholastic standpoint, as with Chomsky) at the origin of discourse, or a metapractice (law, in the case of a number of ethnologists, who have inclined to juridism, or, as with Lévi-Strauss, the rules of kinship with the aid of play on the different senses of the world 'rule', which Wittgenstein has taught us to distinguish) at the origin of practices.[101]

Chomsky's epistemocentrism, mentioned above, depends on the assumption that practice (performance) is reduced in his vision to implementation (application) of the rules of grammar. Knowledge of practice is therefore reduced to knowledge of rules. This state of affairs results in *scholastic fallacy*, which „consists in injecting *meta*-into discourses and practices".[102] Epistemocentrism is reducing practical reason to theoretical reason, disregarding or even overlooking the logic governing practice.[103] Bourdieu hints at the – essential- difference between practical knowledge – reasonable reason – and the scientific knowledge – scholastic, theoretical, reasoning reason – that is generated in autonomous fields."[104]

Whereas in the 20th century social sciences were still (as in the 19th century) developed in the spirit of epistemocentrism and, consequently, fell into traps of dualisms (objectivism – subjectivism/constructivism), naturalism – idealism/anti-realism, structure – agency, learning subject – acting subject, study – action, involvement – neutrality, value – fact etc.), the proceeding decay of epistemological fundamentalism engendered a need to verify epistemocentrism and fill the "epistemological gap" in social sciences. This need should be construed as the growing conviction among late 20th century sociologists that social processes and phenomena should be investigated with regard to their intelligibility character. At the same time scholars lacked a research apparatus free from the epistemocentric twist.

Polish sociologist Helena Kozakiewicz, perfectly aware of the problem with epistemocentrism, diagnoses it using other terms than Bourdieu. She proposes a critique of sociological reason, meant to be "a critique of cognitive helplessness permeating thinking about society, thinking shaped by

---

101 Bourdieu, *Pascalian Meditations*, pp. 52-53.
102 Bourdieu, *Practical Reason*, pp. 130-131.
103 Pierre Bourdieu, *Le sens pratique*, Les Éditions de Minuit, Paris 1980, pp. 135-165.
104 Bourdieu, *Pascalian Meditations*, p. 50.

the ideology of objectivist academic science, supported with the authority of the great Kant, rooted in Descartes's *Meditations* and *Discourse on the Method*.[105] She understands critique not in the Kantian meaning, but in the meaning proposed by Adorno and Feyerabend, as "a critique of *ideology* masking the structural properties of that "reason", the very properties that actually enable this reason to perform the function postulated by the ideology".[106]

Kozakiewicz points at problems of sociology stemming from the domination of epistemocentrism and epistemological fundamentalism. She states:

> [...] socialisation as subject of sociology and social philosophy refuses to be epistemologised within the developed so far "epistemological figures". Pre-epistemologicality of social learning (the inability to cross the "epistemological threshold") is of structural nature, not historical. We should say then, that the discourse of socialisation is beyond epistemology from the point of view of traditional epistemology; in its conceptual apparatus acquiring knowledge about social reality is not possible to capture in a discourse and therefore it must remain a non-discursive area.[107]

Using Foucault's language, Kozakiewicz points out the limitations of applying "epistemological figures" of traditional, classical epistemology to social sciences. She stresses essential problems of sociology shaped within the classical epistemology paradigm, which are the lack of theoretical concept of contemporary world and the lack of an adequate tool to construct such a concept. The problem lies in the fact that science formed according to the modern ideal of science (a modern *episteme*[108]) and, as such, it

---

105 Helena Kozakiewicz, *Krytyka rozumu socjologicznego*, in: *Racjonalność, nauka, społeczeństwo (A Critique of Sociological Reason*, in: *Rationality, Science, Society)*, ed. Helena Kozakiewicz, Edmund Mokrzycki, Marek J. Siemek, PWN, Warszawa 1989, p. 361. See also Helena Kozakiewicz, *Zwierciadło społecznego świata (The Mirror of the Social World)*, PWN, Warszawa 1991.
106 Kozakiewicz, *Krytyka rozumu socjologicznego*, p. 361.
107 Helena Kozakiewicz, *Epistemologia tradycyjna a problemy współczesności. Punkt widzenia socjologa (Traditional Epistemology and Problems of Contemporaneity. A Sociologist's Point of View)*, in: *Borderlands of Epistemology*, ed. Józef Niżnik, Wydawnictwo IFiS PAN, Warszawa 1992, p. 178.
108 Cf. Foucault, *The Order of Things*, pp. 375-422.

cannot perform an analysis of the contemporary world. The latter not only forces it into another kind of thinking about knowledge, but it also puts it in other contexts in social realities of late/post-/modernity.[109] "Knowledge" construed philosophically according to patterns of early modern epistemology, emerges here as an obstacle to growth of knowledge in social sciences.

In Foucault's language, used by Kozakiewicz, it is a situation where these sciences cannot cross the threshold of epistemologisation. Foucault says:

> When in the operation of a discursive formation, a group of statements is articulated, claims to validate (even unsuccessfully) norms of verification and coherence, and when it exercises a dominant function (as a model, a critique, or a verification) over knowledge, we will say that the discursive formation crosses a *threshold of epistemologization*. When the epistemological figure thus outlined obeys a number of formal criteria, when its statements comply not only with archaeological rules of formation, but also with certain laws for the construction of propositions, we will say that it has crossed a *threshold of scientificity*.[110]

The threshold of scientificity separates the sphere of cognition as if "from the bottom", extracting discursive practices in their individuality and independence (here knowledge crosses the threshold of positivity), and "from the top", by the threshold of scientificity marked by the presence of formal rules to construct sentences of science.[111] A specific discursive formation, having its objects and its ways of seeing these objects, crosses the threshold of epistemologisation when it determines norms of cognition on its own. A discourse, understood in the vein of Foucault's philosophy, is any set of utterances bounded otherwise than only by the rules of language.[112] Each

---

109 Cf. Kozakiewicz, *Epistemologia tradycyjna a problemy współczesności*, p. 159.
110 Michel Foucault, *The Archaeology of Knowledge and the Discourse on the Language*, trans. Alan Mark Sheridan-Smith, Pantheon Books, New York 1972, p. 187.
111 Cf. Foucault, *The Archaeology of Knowledge*, pp. 186-189.
112 Literature, law, science etc. are all forms of discourse. Thus to understand literature, a legal or scientific text, it is not enough to just know the language. Understanding them depends on the ability to distinguish one discourse from another by discursive regularities, as opposed to purely linguistic ones. In order not to confuse e.g. the tale of Little Red Riding Hood with a legal document, one needs specific discursive competences, not only linguistic ones.

discourse is governed by normative conditions of utterance consistency and is constituted by regular reference to the same phenomena. It does not have to be a scientific discipline, it can be, for example, penal sentencing. The normative history of discourses is determined not by their object or method, but by the vector of utterance articulation accuracy.

Kozakiewicz's thesis is the following: contemporary rationality has created a discourse on social reality, that is, sociology, and it has been done so that it cannot properly examine this reality because of its involvement in this reality. Sociology is the best expression of modernity's self-awareness, at the same time revealing all its imperfections. Kozakiewicz sees the reflective attitude of thought in its sociological application as unable to give an adequate representation. If the representing is part of or a product of the represented, it will never represent precisely and remains in a relation of metonymy or metaphor, or even a symptom. We could add that in social reality as such also lies a centre of resistance to epistemologisation attempts. For we can artificially and erroneously mark this threshold of epistemologisation by imposing unsuitable forms of expressing truths concerning reality. This exactly happens in a social science dominated by epistemocentrism. But can social reality and human practices be captured in a theory without losing their ontic status, the practical sense?

Hence epistemocentrism is an obstacle of sorts and a source of social sciences' recurring crises. It happens whenever their own scholastic disposition is treated as an obvious departure point for their work. This blocks analysis of involvements in social being, necessary in sociology, its social condition. Therefore we need a new perspective, which would include ontic pluralism of social world, namely, that there are multiple axiologically normative orders (human worlds) and none of them is (absolutely) privileged in relation to others. That perspective should also acknowledge plurality, that is, multiple subjects-actors in the world. The pluralism of knowledge should be accepted too (as Aristotle did, but taking into account the specific character of the modern world and modern kinds of knowledge). These three kinds of pluralism (multiplicity of worlds, people and epistemic forms of knowledge) meet in the subject seen as an agent, who is the "builder" of their own subjectivity, of social world and knowledge of this world. Here is the fact that every social theory must acknowledge in its considerations: subjects are simultaneously objects for themselves. As long as this is seen as an insurmountable epistemological problem, such categories as "rationality", "intersubjectivity" and "objectivity" are treated exclusively as properties of methodical study, as opposed to attributes of social order, where knowledge may have its social dimension.

4. Truth in social sciences

Truth, especially in the 20th century, the era when epistemological fundamentalism started to crumble, became a highly debatable category. Its rival – certainty – had inadvertently risen to power in the shadows. Since the advent of early modern philosophy the proposed strict procedures of verification and falsification had defended the line of demarcation between science and other kinds of knowledge in a way hugely risky for the universal value of truth. The "human truth",[113] the truth of aesthetic experience, truth as an effect of intuitive cognition, truth as a requirement of being a subject: all of these modes of understanding were marginalised when certainty (the value of the method) became the most pursued value of knowledge in the belief that it would ascertain the truth as well. Paradoxically, truth has then become an obstacle for the shape of new, young and methodologically immature knowledge, unable to meet often very strict, arbitrarily established criteria. The modern era is a breakthrough in history also because it methodically erects a barrier between truth as a value and knowledge as a fact. It opens for knowledge (Columbus's and Galileo's discoveries), but only where it seeks its new formula devised by a new method. Effectiveness of research, growth of knowledge, as consequences of making the method a key aspect of scientific study, have become so attractive values that either epistemological replacements of truth began to be sought or its new philosophical formulas. In philosophy and sciences the category of truth was attempted to be replaced with certainty of method and obviousness of acknowledgement (Descartes), in the 19th century with objectivity, in the 20th century with intersubjectivity (understood as scholars' communicational consent in reaching the truth), as well as consistency, coherence (coherence theory of truth), convention

---

113 Cf. Detienne, *The Masters of Truth in Archaic Greece*, pp. 35-38.

(the content of notions is conventionally determined: conventional truth theory), verification (logical positivism), efficiency and usefulness (pragmatistic theory of truth) etc. It has even been tried to eliminate it from scientific discourse altogether (deflationary or redundancy theory of truth). This epistemological anxiety (not to say: crisis of fundamentalism) is also related to the rise of modern knowledge of society, that is, of social sciences.

Since the times when the discourse of truth was impropriated by philosophy,[114] truth has undoubtedly had its monumental place in Western intellectual traditions, despite criticism addressed, especially nowadays, at purely aspect-oriented logical and semantic conceptualisation of truth. Nevertheless, in humanistic and social sciences, since they appeared, truth is a problematic category, mainly, it seems, because of its epistemocentric location.[115]

The problem with truth in social sciences emerges because in natural sciences, which serve as a model for many scholars, the concept of truth is not so overtly entangled in values lying beyond the sphere of knowledge. Moreover, even when cognitive and, for example, utilitarian (technological) values are in evident accordance in the area of natural study, its epistemologists most often see only casual convergence, as opposed to a necessary relation between these values. Hence, in natural sciences and philosophy concerning them, conviction of truth as a value is prevalent, truth which does not require any additional justification beyond the area of intellect.

In modern times, mainly because of relations between science and technology, the awareness of the conflict between truth and certainty is shaping. This conflict is occasionally described in a radical manner, as a dilemma of choice between these values.[116] Limitations are pointed at,

---

114 Cf. Detienne, *The Masters of Truth in Archaic Greece*, pp. 89-106.
115 Thought critical towards this location begins seemingly with Hegel's philosophy, and in modern times it is taken up by Heidegger, Gadamer and Foucault. What is important, the four mentioned philosophers are driven in this criticism by an ontological motivation.
116 This is how I interpret the radicalism of science philosophy labelled with the *against method* slogan.

imposing such understanding of truth on other values of science.[117] Thus the problem concerns choice between a value which is truth, and other cognitive values, but it is also sometimes extended to border areas between truth and values unrelated to knowledge, such as virtue, solidarity, freedom, use.

Epistemology founded on "methodologism" and its order does not comply with modern reality. Truth can be the principal and ordering value of knowledge only when we have a contemplative attitude towards knowledge. The very idea of knowledge "application", in its technological meaning, distorts the epistemological order based on truth. This happens to an even greater extent when knowledge is involved practically in the life of individuals and communities.

Philosophies of modernity most often question not so much the possibility to reach the truth, as its primacy to other values. So they announce the end of truth as a prime value in knowledge and the end of epistemology as a theory of knowledge based on the primacy of truth. Rorty's statement that nowadays we witness the demise of "ultimate truth" provides a good example.[118] Hence, in the new context of modern reality, the reality of new, non-contemplative roles of knowledge, we must ask a post-Kantian question: what opportunities are there in modernity to conceptualise truth not on the foundation of its epistemological primacy, but on its participation in social life? It is a critical question, concerning conditions of truth's existence and functioning in social life and in scientific discourse on that life.

Therefore, the main critical question asked within social ontoepistemology is as follows: why is the epistemologically established idea of truth so oppressive towards social sciences? The key to the answer lies in Foucault's thought: being a subject and having the truth (as opposed to truth as such) must form a hereby described union. If you do not accept the obligation to acknowledge truth, if you are not in possession of some

---

117 Cf. Amsterdamski, *The Sources of the Crisis of the Modern Ideal of Sciences*, pp. 79-100.

118 Cf. Richard Rorty, *Zmierzch prawdy ostatecznej i narodziny kultury literackiej (The Decline of Redemptive Truth and the Rise of a Literary Culture)*, „Teksty Drugie: teoria literatury, krytyka, interpretacja" 2003, no. 6 (84), pp. 113-130.

truth about yourself and about others, then you cannot exist either for yourself, or for others, as a thinking and acting subject. One cannot be a subject and a participant of interactional social order with no relevance to the fact that one is a knowing subject and a subject assessing knowledge, hence – a creator of ways to verify truth. As modern knowledge is organised mainly in scientific form and people are subjects of knowledge, the history of knowledge, the genealogy of a modern subject and the history of meaning systems are tightly related. The epistemocentric discourse on truth, apart from all the purposes it can serve, also plays a role of a discourse blurring the above relations.

However, every person who takes part in the culture of Western society, Foucault says, is obliged by this culture to know themselves and expressing the truth about themselves.[119] This is a very important statement. It says that on the basis of social sciences truth becomes a reflective category. It means that truth refers to the one who judges, speaks, acts, and at the same time to the one who, producing truth, forms a specific, subjective way of their being. Truth is a constitutive category for subjectivity. Thanks to it, one can be recognised by others as a subject. This way the old philosophical problem is revived in the shape of the question: is truth discovered or produced? That is why also in the area of social sciences attempts have been made to find such a way of seeing a human being, in which the truth about the person precedes this person's awareness of the bond with truth. This allows for an understanding of truth which is uncontroversial within epistemocentrism. But then truth ceases to be a reflective and ontological category. This concept has affected the lot of humanistic and social sciences. I mean scientistic, positivist or not, concepts of sociology and its subject matter. This solution has always been a source of trouble for those researchers, who, like Foucault, treated truth as a reflective category, entangled in ontology, in the belief that eliminating these characteristics would remove the meaning of truth in the area of social sciences, that is,

---

119 Cf. Michel Foucault, *Subjectivity and Truth*, in: Michel Foucault, *The Politics of Truth*, ed. Sylvère Lotringer, trans. Lysa Hochroth & Catherine Porter, Semiotext(e), Los Angeles 2007, pp. 147-167.

its reference to the thinking subject both in the ontological and epistemic aspect.[120]

Another troublesome issue related to truth in the area of social sciences is their sensitivity to time, the role of the passing of time, limiting validity of truths they utter. It is not so much about how the passing of time transforms social sciences' objects of interest, changing truths about what was in the light of truths about what is. It is more about the role of referring knowledge to the future, in which this knowledge wants to participate.

Processes of social life run under the pressure of goals assumed by acting subjects, so the imagined goals are largely determined by means to achieve them. As in every practice, the efficiency of their relation depends on the justness of the goals and the certainty of the means. So social sciences are forced to analyse ways of experiencing the future, ways to emotionally and intellectually judge visions and assumed methods of practical and provisional corrections of actions with the purposes in mind. In natural sciences what is confronts what used to be. Unlike that, in social sciences one departs from what is and goes towards what can be (what most often expresses their critical aspect in showing that what is could be otherwise[121]) or should be (the axiological aspect). Using the Aristotelian participative model of social sciences, we could say they concern what can be otherwise in such a way that it can be brought to reality in the future. How then can we speak about truth in theories meant to be applied to the future? This question seems especially significant in view of the changeability and dynamics of sociology's subject matter and the involvement of theory. In fact, social theories are also practices of sorts. Moreover, the question is important for acknowledging sociology's disciplinary autonomy.

---

120 "If someone wanted to be a philosopher but didn't ask himself the question, 'What is knowledge?', or, 'What is truth?', in what sense could one say he was a philosopher? And for all that I may like to say I'm not a philosopher, nonetheless if my concern is with truth then I am still a philosopher." Michel Foucault, *Question on Geography*, in Foucault, *Power/Knowledge...* p. 66.

121 The critical aspect understood this way was developed mainly in the Frankfurt school.

Special trouble with social sciences is related to adoption (often with no objections) of concepts of truth (as well as models of scientificity) directly from natural sciences, along with all the epistemocentric burden. This is visible in their history. Jan Hudzik, reconstructing concepts of truth in social sciences, points at two opposing concepts adopted in these sciences: the one related to naturalism and the one related to constructivism. Naturalists "sport the idea of »naked facts« and aspire to universal truths", while constructivists "link what is factual with what is socially established". Within the constructivist concept he distinguishes three approaches: the hermeneutical one links truth to interpretation and understanding, the political one (within political epistemology) treats truth as a relation of social domination and subjugation, and the aesthetic one seeks truth by "describing and explaining social life in terms of analogies to symbolic forms, like a game, a text, a language or a story".[122]

The review made by Hudzik hints that representatives of social sciences cannot break free from the dualistic thinking: readymade reality against created reality, the objective order of things and subjective creative acts, static structure and creative agency, truth discovered (objective) and constructed (subjective), facts and values etc.

In order to avoid these dualisms in social sciences, we should suspend epistemocentrism, get out of the cognitive context towards social life and experience which is shaped by it. Gadamer provides a good example of such orientation in social sciences. In the 1953 article *Truth in the Human Sciences* he says:

> Instead of obvious or generally convincing results the philosopher is called upon to bring to language the questionable [*das Bedenkliche*] and that which calls for thoughtful consideration [*das Nachdenkliche*] that offers itself in the work of the human sciences to those who think.[123]

We must agree with him, however with the reservation that doubt and uncertainty are the mere beginning of all rational thinking. Since *dubito*

---

122 Cf. Jan P. Hudzik, *Prawda w naukach społecznych (Truth in Social Sciences)*, *Prawda (The Truth)*, ed. Damian Leszczyński, Wydawnictwo Uniwersytetu Wrocławskiego, Wrocław 2011, p. 364.
123 Hans-Georg Gadamer, *Truth in the Human Sciences*, in: Brice R. Wachterhauser (ed.), *Hermeneutics and Truth*, Northwestern University Press, 1994, p. 25.

always precedes *cogito*, a mind devoid of doubt is not an independent mind, it is deprived of individuality, like a calculator. Doubt is inscribed in social and humanistic research as a component of specifically human reality. In this reality not only rapid developments make formulating fixed laws impossible, but above all the role of "free choice" (outside causality inherent in scientistic understanding of needs, like the need to eat, sleep, do something and play with something). Meanwhile, in natural sciences doubt and uncertainty sound like summons to settle as quickly as possible (in experiments) what would be a universal and unconditionally valid fixed law for all objects "of a given type". Humanist study, contrary to naturalist, concerns principally the exceptional, as opposed to the common, „and makes the human sciences so significant and worthy of questioning for us".[124] This is probably because the development of humanity proceeds in the way of individual "mutations" of behaviour and action, accepted by others and subsequently mimicked by the community, which results in perpetuation in the form of rules.

How are social sciences scientific? – Gadamer asks. This surely does not depend on methodical investigation of human matters. Do they fulfil the need to know? Are they a quest for truth? Yes, although it is difficult to prove, because human sciences reveal the historical sense of measures and methods, which in epistemology may be considered relativism, and on its fringes it borders nihilism.[125] The path towards truth in human sciences, according to Gadamer, is different than in natural sciences. Here the authority of the (wizened) reason is binding, with the imperative "to stand in tradition and to heed it".[126] Truth is conditioned historically and co-created, co-thought, co-acknowledged. The elder's authority is only a metaphor of tradition and conservatism, relying on older and verified forms of thinking and acting, resulting inevitably in the community's continuous existence. In social life it does not suffice to affirm that something exists, we need an answer to the question: why does it persist, although it does not have to? Why is it like this, while it could be otherwise? What causes/

---

124 Gadamer, *Truth in the Human Science*, p. 26.
125 Gadamer, *Truth in the Human Science*, p. 27.
126 Gadamer, *Truth in the Human Science*, p. 29.

creates the social "being"? What keeps it, in a necessary way, in existence, enforcing or weakening it?

Since the early modernity natural sciences have been considered a source of economic success, evidently enforcing "being", persistence and even expansion and dominance of an economically active community. In the name of common rationality and purposefulness they encourage human sciences to support the same goal. In practice this goal is secured by the scientistic certificate of truth, which is factuality, predictability, steerability and... technical creativity of phenomena (as in each laboratory). Scientism, paradigmatically embracing sociology, defends the stance that truth about social life is discovered and can be used in practice for sociotechnical inventions. Meanwhile, the humanist approach defends the stance that truth is co-created, even in hyperscientific collectives and in all other communities.

> They [human sciences] cannot release themselves from the responsibility which stems from the fact that they have an effect. Against all manipulation of opinion through a controlled public realm in the modern world, they exercise an immediate influence regarding family and school on an ever-growing humanity. Where truth is in them, they are marked by the trace of an inextinguishable freedom.[127]

Human sciences: „[they] are *logoi,* speech, »only« speech"[128] – here Gadamer quotes Plato, stressing the thought that the essence of social sciences is investigating texts and live acts of communication. Gadamer's statements can be extended. Then they refer not only to texts, but also to actions. We can ask: in what way is activity in social sciences, especially sociology, specific? Can we speak about truth in these sciences and how can we do it?

Gadamer gives truth an ontological character and introduces axiological motifs to the discourse of truth. His concept of truth is developed by Barbara Tuchańska, in the ontological vein. In her book *Dlaczego prawda? (Why Truth?)* she adopts a broad perspective: a hermeneutical one [„philosophical considerations of truth are made from inside the situation ..."], ontological-ontic („truth does not boil down to trueness") and

---

127 Gadamer, *Truth in the Human Science,* p. 31.
128 Gadamer, *Truth in the Human Science,* p. 32.

axiological ("the meaning of truth, trueness and truthfulness for people").
The author says:

> This perspective should then be holistic, not one-sided; ontological, not logical
> and semantic; socio-historical, not individual and hermeneutical, not epistemo-
> logical. [...] Analysis in this spirit allows to avoid objectivization of truth and
> trueness, i.e. treating truth as the state of Being, and trueness as a relation be-
> tween the vehicle of truth and the state of affairs (not containing truth). It allows
> to capture truth and untruth as ontological structures of our being and show
> that truth and trueness, along with untruth and falseness, are inextricably linked
> with dialogue, language and interpretational tradition, as well as with social
> institutions and normative systems. All of this means that they are irreducibly
> historical and community-based.[129]

Since knowledge is an ontic component of society's structure and function,
which are the subject matter of onto-epistemology, considerations appre-
ciating this knowledge brought into life requires recognising modes of its
social acceptance. Thus while appealing to the truth as a value is common,
its actual meaning includes benefit, functionality, effectivity, as well as
compliance with the agreement. Knowledge can be passed in unverbalised
ways, as mimicking or pedagogical-educational procedures, as experience
in different acts of participation leading to attainment of a specific skill,
as well as cultural empathy and identity. Hence it always reached beyond
epistemocentric approaches. In this context, after Heidegger, we can remind the multiplicity of meanings contained in the Greek *aletheia*. Indeed,
before the birth of epistemology people evaluated knowledge and included
it (or rejected) in practical action or social behaviour.

---

129 Barbara Tuchańska, *Dlaczego prawda? Prawda jako wartość w sztuce, nauce i
codzienności (Why Truth? Truth as a Value in Art, Science, and Everyday Life)*,
Wydawnictwo Poltext, Warszawa 2012, pp. 16-17.

Chapter III A Social Onto-Epistemology

Rationality, objectivity, intersubjectivity, since early modernity have been perceived as primarily epistemological categories, above all meant to characterise knowledge, possibly subjects of cognition or these subjects' actions. Epistemocentrism, characteristic for early modern science and philosophy, as well as epistemological fundamentalism and representationism supporting it, have contributed to such strictly epistemological narrowing of these terms' meanings. Nowadays, in the face of social sciences' established presence in the order of knowledge, and in the face of changing roles of knowledge in social life, these notions understood purely epistemologically simply become an anachronism, a troublesome and useless excess, or even an epistemological obstacle preventing proper explanation of and understanding social worlds, leading to misunderstandings and reductionisms. Nowadays neither knowledge (or science) is what it was in the times when epistemocentrism flourished, nor its participation in reality forged by social processes is the same as before. Hence the need to question epistemocentrism and fill the "epistemological gap" left after the collapse of epistemological fundamentalism. Having overcome the epistemocentric point of view on science, cognition and reality, we face a different perspective of understanding and use of the above notions: the path of onto-epistemology. The need emerges for ontological reflection in social sciences. Sociology is, *nolens volens*, a theory of intersubjectivity, rationality and objectivity construed as correlates of both knowledge and being, especially being in society.

Of course, the issues of rationality, objectivity and intersubjectivity are not new in the area of philosophical considerations. These notions gained special importance in modern thought tradition, as questions about rationality of knowledge and its subject, objectivity of investigation (knowledge) and intersubjectivity of assumed positions and convictions, earned their place in philosophy. As early as the end of the 19th century a new context of these problems began to form. Rationality is a category without which it is difficult to even imagine doing any science (not only sociology).[130]

---

130 On the rationality of science see Monika Walczak, *Racjonalność nauki.*

However, rationality is not just a synonym of scientificity, nor is it a synonym of value in a scientific method. It is not only a category describing broadly understood human activities, but it can also be seen as the intelligible order of being in which people take part, similarly as it was in ancient philosophy, where the understanding of the term "rationality" was identified with the term *logos*. It is especially worthwhile to remind that *logos* was a concept organising thinking about the world even before any philosophy and initially it referred to law (rules ordering and governing the mutability and diversity of *polis*) and hence a socially rooted category. The genius of the first Greek wisemen depended on projecting these rules on the universe, which since then has aspired to the name of *Cosmos*. To understand the order of the world philosophers ontologised such terms as "debt and guilt" (in Anaximander's intuitions of nature's law and justice), "love and dissent" (in Empedocles's thought), taken from areas of thought that we identify today in categories of rationality, objectivity and intersubjectivity. Analogies for the laws of nature and ontological structure of being had their source in life and social experience. This very social life (the other side of the analogy), in turn, was not reciprocated either by ontology, or epistemology.[131]

In modern times the notion of *subiectum* became significant for understanding rationality: rationality was then construed above all as a certain order of subjective representations, individual, though formed by civilisation. Since empirical human sciences emerged, including sociology, the notion of rationality has been used as such a concept of order that is neither purely objective nor subjective. The order of sorts, sought in social sciences, becomes a domain of verifying the general meaning of rationality. Rationality as a critical concept, devoid of direct activity, is that very

---

Problemy, koncepcje, argumenty (*Rationality of Science. Problems, Concepts, Arguments*), Towarzystwo Naukowe KUL, Lublin 2006.

131 Social experience and knowledge, gathered in tradition for millennia (socio-*doxa vs* later sociology), since presocratic beginnings has been inscribed in the drama of King Lear, who endowed his philosophical daughters with principles and founding thoughts for the development of their dukedoms, being himself deprived of possessions and prerogatives.

concept which is attributed with the ability to reveal the sense of modernity as a special order.

On the sociological ground, all these assumptions which allowed us to overlook the entanglements of "experience", "subject", "knowledge", "rationality", "objectivity" and similar categories in their extra-cognitive meanings have proven debatable. These extra-cognitive meanings are important in view of other categories, showing their usefulness on the ground of social sciences, like "interaction", "co-operation", "communication", "action", "intersubjectivity".

Each of the three distinguished categories at least once in sociology's short history has played a role of an important idea, around which research was organised and the value and meaning of sociology's scientificity were determined. Rationality of social orders is a central thread to Weber's, Parsons's, Lukács's, Garfinkel's and Habermas's sociology. "Objectivity" allowed Durkheim to organise principal problems in "sociology of social facts". The notion of intersubjectivity played a significant, motivating role in formulating the conceptual apparatus and problems of phenomenological sociology (Alfred Schütz, Aron Gurwitsch, Richard Zaner, Thmas Luckmann, Peter Berger) and provided a foundation for symbolic interactionism (Georg Herbert Mead, Herbert Blumer, Erving Goffman).

Modern 20th-century sociology is characterised by the need to combine all these categories in one, common theoretical context. This approach to sociology was promoted by Habermas (along with Niklas Luhmann, Pierre Bourdieu and Norbert Elias), and before him by Znaniecki. Specificity of such approaches (shared also by Giddens and Taylor) lies in the conviction of an active role played by intellectual factors in social life and in awareness of the influence exerted by social reality on theoretical approaches proposed by sociology. That is why the right platform for considering the issues of rationality, objectivity and intersubjectivity is situating them in the context of social reality. It is the source area of activities (co-operation, communication and fight), and secondarily of shaping relatively changeable intellectual content of "rationality", "objectivity" and "intersubjectivity", and as a consequence also of such notions as subjectivity, experience, subject.

1. Onto-epistemological specificity of social sciences

Stanisław Ossowski, Florian Znaniecki, Charles Taylor, Pierre Bourdieu – these thinkers do not exhaust the list of those who wrote about peculiarities or specificity of social sciences. Neither their involvement in the critique of epistemocentrism is of the same kind. Some of them, including Ossowski's concept, seem a bit obsolete, especially in reference to social realities of late modernity, which reveal special social part of knowledge. Nowadays the dynamics of social phenomena, their range and pace, can, as never before, reach deep into the social structure and spread into new areas of life. New forms of interpersonal interaction emerge, based on technology and the Internet (*social media*), new forms of experiencing an individual self (e.g. related to gender roles), new forms of collective life (easiness of participation in mass forms of culture). Frequently, these changes concern "axiomatic" social bonds and relations (the primary ones, providing models for others).

Sensitivity to this sort of process makes social sciences an undoubtedly different discourse than natural sciences. Half a century has passed since Ossowski wrote *Special Characteristics of the Social Sciences* and time adds *novum* to the specific character of these sciences. Nowadays we should rather think of their specificity than peculiarity, since peculiarities are characteristics departing from the norm, deviations, paradoxes, irregularities, eccentricities. In this approach, epistemology of these sciences gravitates towards some form of "teratology of knowledge" rather than "disciplinary epistemology", stressing the *species* of some kinds of study and knowledge. Social sciences have earned a significant position among other sciences, their role and importance have been acknowledged, and they are abandoning the discourse of making amends for their insufficiently scientific or marginal position. The role of social sciences in the contemporary, fast-changing world, is determined by two properties of modern life. The first of them is the requirement of far-reaching prospection, foresight into the future of social processes, which stems from the uncertainty as to the direction of changes. The second is the growing part of knowledge in social life environments, which is related to the inevitable technological and political intermediation of late modern forms of participation in social life.

Speaking about the peculiarities of sciences, we would still remain under the power of epistemocentric thinking, that we strive to overcome. That is why the expression of "specificity" is more appropriate than "peculiarity" in reference to social sciences, as specificity points at differences of *species*, while peculiarity hints at individual differences: inimitable, irregular, separate, therefore bizarre and possibly defying understanding. It is time to leave the *Wunderkammer* of social sciences. Sociology is nowadays well-defined as a *species* of science (as every other science). Although this specificity includes scientific investigation of peculiarities, which are individual subjects, free, sometimes unpredictable in their actions, and yet these subjects remain in constant relations with the specificity of a regular group. Thus sociology seeks laws (rules) of relations between individual peculiarities and the specific character of a collective. Consequently, sociology as a science does not have to be peculiar, although it retains its specificity. The peculiarity lies in its subject matter.

Sociology has already stopped wrestling for scientific status in the traditional meaning, that is, a science aiming at strict generality and universality, now it is mainly about gaining autonomy. Autonomy is also important for extra-cognitive reasons: institutional, even commercial. Seemingly, this "autonomy" is a criterion of disciplinary identity secretly rooted in social life. Autonomy fought for with theoretical means is above all needed to pose problems, conduct research, but not necessarily to settle them with no outside assistance. Autonomy is a condition of "institutional subjectification", becoming the source of sociology's goals and the will to pursue them. Historical separations and classifications frequently change and are created *ex post*, often for other than *stricte* scientific purposes. They result in errors and artificiality, while their corrections lead to new divisions, as well as to connecting areas separated in the past (e.g. biophysics, sociobiology, biochemistry).

Sociology is often impropriated by either natural sciences or humanities, radically antagonised and desperately seeking a model of dominant science, which would justify that impropriation. Neither side can do without including social (collective, communitarian) factors in search of scientificity criteria. The best proof is the career of the term "discourse" or "narrative" in humanities. Indispensability of the presence and participation of the social factor in both types of sciences encourages further criticism of previous classifications of what is the living structure of cognition: areas, threads, branches, curios and peculiarities, individuals and groups etc. The inaccurate (often arbitrary and doctrine-driven) division is a sin of philosophy, that, by a "royal decree" established the division into ontology and epistemology. The concept of onto-epistemology is a concept of rejecting former criteria of autonomy and correspondence between subjects and disciplines, based on the idea of substantiality (of the subject or the object of study), in favour of "relations", "kinships" or "interactionality". Epistemocentric demarcation lines in disciplinary study, making up the order built on classifying and exclusive criteria, is replaced by the order organising cognition according to rules "integrating" network links of different problematisations.

Social onto-epistemology always relates ideas such as "trueness", "truth", "objectivity", "intersubjectivity", "rationality", "experience", "subject", "knowledge", to the situation of human life environment. Omission of the human world seems a highly abstract enterprise or just an intellectual experiment conducted on the ground of idealistic or anti-realistic positions. Maybe such experiments bring measurable benefits in the form of, for example, technological development, gaining deeper knowledge in areas directly unrelated to human beings and their environment. On the other hand, I think that the indispensability of onto-epistemology can be proven even when seeking "pure" (scientific) knowledge, manufactured in isolated laboratories and conditions separating from the environment and from life. An investigating subject participates in the investigated entity, and through participation in it, co-constitutes that entity. Knowledge/science not only explains and describes the world, the reality that surrounds us, but it becomes an active participant in life. Social theory which is understood as practice, involved, adjusting practices, interpreting, including reflective self-descriptions and self-definitions (Taylor), creating a logic of practice (Bourdieu), including the humanistic coefficient (Znaniecki), referring to interpretational social practice (Abel, Lenk) and all social theories of onto-epistemological orientation, confirm that. That is why the language of social sciences must be reformulated to capture the specificity of the object, which is a complex of onto-epistemic conditions of each relatively permanent community. Hence there are two kinds of discourse in sociology: philosophical and scientific. The base of the former is the conviction that all scientific knowledge in this area is rooted in experience enclosed within defined boundaries. In this area, human beings' social existence is created and reproduced, as well as discourse. This process includes epistemic reproduction and production. The latter discourse has a critical-epistemological character and stems from the tradition of thought about science often still unfamiliar with links between knowledge and its object, conditions of existence and conditions of cognition related to them, bonds between involvement and distance, both in cognitive and in existential sense of these terms.

The specificity of contemporary social (sociological) theories is understanding new roles of knowledge. Many social researchers, representing different positions, schools, approaches in contemporary social theories seem to understand it. Patrick Baert and Filipe Carreira da Silva write about such an understanding of knowledge on the ground of neopragmatism, „in which it neither represents nor mirrors any outside world, but constitutes an active intervention".[132] Knowledge, as the authors see it, is involved and of self-referential character, thus it is targeted at revealing premises lying at its foundations. This approach abandons cognition construed as contemplation of objects and gives it a sense of action. In turn, Anthony Giddens, the author of structuration theory, sees the specificity of sociology and social sciences in "double hermeneutics", by which he understands "mutual interpretative interplay between social science and those whose activities compose its subject matter". Further on, he says: „The theories and findings of the social sciences cannot be kept wholly separate from the universe of meaning and action which they are about."[133]

Let us recall then: social sciences are rooted in a certain order of social activities that has fostered conditions for reflection on that order. Therefore they are inevitably involved, entangled into orders of actions which

---

132 Patrick Baert, Filipe Carreira da Silva, *Social Theory in the Twentieth Century and Beyond*, Polity Press, Cambridge 2010, (*Preface to the Polish Edition*, Zakład Wydawniczy NOMOS, Kraków 2013, p. XXIII).

133 Anthony Giddens, *The Construction of Society. Outline of the Theory of Structuration*, University of California Press, Berkeley and Los Angeles 1984, pp. xxxii-xxxiii.

are the object of study. That is why from the point of view of social onto-epistemology the following questions gain importance: how is knowledge about society created? What are its social roles? What is the specific character of its presence in social reality when it is that reality that is being described?

Knowledge is a social achievement. Hence its interpersonal character is significant. Knowledge exists, transforms subjects or their actions, it constitutes ground for experience or its consequence, when it is shared. Knowledge exists in the same way as language does: it is not obtained "from nature", and its durability, functionality, efficiency depends on the interpersonal. Therefore it depends on the coincidence of different factors to yield acceptance. Knowledge as a reservoir of social experience can only be learnt (not heard of!) from others. To teach, according to Aristotle, means to internalise the social pattern of participation, hence to forge the way of joining a collective action, thus making a long-exercised habit a "second nature". If ancient philosophers maintained that teaching is performed in the triad: *mathesis, didaskalia, askesis*, they were convinced that motivation to learn of the "how to do it" type is important and, above all, a consequence of that motivation: exercise. In this sense learnt, durable and specific forms of being in a collective, repeatedly renewed intergenerational cultural conventions, form a kind of knowledge socially stored and preserved, not only "rendered" to individuals as information. This way knowledge reshapes an individual's relations with the world of objects and with people and it acquires an ontic status. The knowledge that a philosopher, Heidegger, discovered in "handiness", and another philosopher, Gadamer, in superstitions (or preconceptions), is always social knowledge and it is undetachable from human activity and human environment. It is an essential adhesive of subjectivity, that is revealed in self-narrations, a distinction of a whole group's specificity, when it enables identification with others, it constitutes the "society's being". It is the lowest level where the ontic blends with the epistemic.

Three notions: rationality, objectivity and intersubjectivity play an essential role in the social onto-epistemology project as especially significant for sociology and other social sciences, and at the same time carrying a hefty burden of epistemocentrism. Thus regaining their more complex, onto-epistemological sense, is an important goal of the project I call social onto-epistemology.

2. Onto-epistemology of rationality

It is difficult to imagine doing any science (not only sociology) without the category of rationality. Without it neither would it be possible to describe human thinking, nor activity. It is a key idea for philosophy and for science, for theory and practice, for broadly understood human actions (mental, non-mental, communicative, expressive, symbolic etc.) Rationality is not a synonym of scientificity, as epistemocentrics could imagine, or even a synonym of the value carried by scientific method, since it characterises widely understood (not only cognitive) human actions. In the Western philosophical tradition it has counted among basic subjects of philosophical considerations, it has been connected with the question of being, of the foundations of knowledge, of the human being's characteristics as a species, about people's widely understood activity. In modern times it has been associated with socially produced reality orders: with cultural orders. *Logos* and *ratio* were synonymic terms used in antiquity, understood mainly as the intelligible order of being. For so construed rationality I have devised the term of substantial rationality.[134] In early modernity the term *subiectum* belonged to the broad environment of ideas from which the sense of rationality was derived, by rationality understanding a certain order of subjective (produced by subjects) representations. Rationality is a complex of principles subjugating phenomena to immanent rules of Pure Reason, principles establishing the space of valid cognition and marking the boundaries of intelligible representation. I call this kind of rationality procedural.[135]

---

134 Cf. Mariola Kuszyk-Bytniewska, *Rationality as an Onto-epistemological Category*, in: *Етносоціологічний та епістемологічний дискурс у науковому просторі* [*Ethnosociological and Epistemological Discourse in Scientific Space*], eds. Volodymyr Yevtukh, Ryszard Radzik, Ganna Kisla, Інститут соціології, психології та соціальних комунікацій Національного педагогічного університету імені М. П. Драгоманова, Kiev 2013, pp. 246-257.

135 Cf. Kuszyk-Bytniewska, *Rationality as an Onto-epistemological Category*, p. 248.

Criteria and ways of distinguishing problems related to rationality are multiple. To refer to Polish philosophy, we could recall Barbara Skarga's division. She distinguished three main ideas of rationality in the history of European culture: metaphysical, scientistic and technological.[136] Zbigniew Kuderowicz distinguished only two models of rationality: methodological (epistemological) and axiological.[137] Klemens Szaniawski separated rationality of thinking (regarding it as autonomous) from rationality of action (seeing it as exclusively instrumental).[138]

The discovery of rationality, the invention of proof and justification, was a shock in the world of *polis*: in the world reigned by authoritative and causative word, whose credibility was based on likelihood. Rationality, when we capture its sense retrospectively, historically, is a vehicle of thought ruled by the regime of intersubjectivity. Its discovery reveals previously unknown power of discourse linked to the replacement of word-power (authoritative word) or word-conviction (opinion) with word-reason (argument). In this way rationality became one of the powers of discourse, distinguishable from authoritative word and persuasive word. Mythology, fabular and dogmatically conservative, justifiably removed by Plato from his state, gave way to rational discourse, in part appropriated by philosophy. *Logos* was gradually pushing *mythos* away. The power of rational discourse became the subject of research concerning its limits and its forms, as it was discourse directed towards an utterly different manner and order of thinking in communication. Instead of narrative and fabular coherence of authoritative or lyrical word, rationality introduced the balance of credibility between the proposed thesis, initially even the most preposterous, and the sum of arguments supporting it logically. Philosophy and science form an area of culture rooted in this discovery. Therefore the part of rationality in all sorts and areas of philosophy and science is

136 Cf. Barbara Skarga, *Trzy idee racjonalności* (*Three Ideas of Rationality*), „Studia Filozoficzne" 1983, no. 5-6, pp. 17-37.
137 Cf. Zbigniew Kuderowicz, *Dwie tradycje i dwa modele racjonalności* (*Two Traditions and Two Models of Rationality*), „Studia Filozoficzne" 1983, no. 5-6, pp. 254-259.
138 Cf. Klemens Szaniawski, *Racjonalność jako wartość* (*Rationality as a Value*), „Studia Filozoficzne" 1983, no. 5-6, pp. 7-15.

only natural. Rationality is the most universal and the most abstract way of winning the audience both in ontology, epistemology, ethics, anthropology and its other genres, and in all scientific disciplines.

That is why "rationality" is one of few philosophical terms that have survived the aftermath of the "Cartesian revolution" and it has retained the ontic-epistemic irregularity of its meaning. However, the sense of substantial rationality, with its reduction of the category of substance to *Cogito*, has also narrowed. Devoid of the context of social communication, it has been relegated to the domain of subjectivity. It has been made an "innate", "subjective" disposition of an individual person, whereas now it is being painstakingly pulled away from there and returned to the primordial place and the role of mediation, "being between" individuals. The onto-epistemological duality does not refer to such a term as "subject" or "subjectivity". In its history, the former has travelled the way from a strictly ontological concept of Aristotle's metaphysics (*hypokeimenon*) to the epistemological and critical idea (*subiectum*) of modern philosophy. The latter has swapped meanings with its antonym: "objectivity".[139] Nevertheless, the word "rational" or "rationality" is quite commonly used both to describe certain ontic structures and as a qualification of certain cognitive structures. Though, in Habermas's words, whereas „the rationality of beliefs and actions is a theme usually dealt with in philosophy", „among the social sciences sociology is most likely to link its basic concepts to the rationality problematic".[140] Following this statement, we must note that it is concrete, empirical reality, as the soil of social worlds, that is a primordial, source area of rationality formation, both as a theoretical concept and a certain category of social life. It is fair to say that the problems of rationality are inscribed in the very project of sociology as a scientific discipline, with respect to the subject matter and with respect to methodology. Rationality is not only an epistemological qualification and it is sensibly referred not only to entities of thought: arguments, theories, methods and other intellectual forms. People, actions, social institutions

---

139 I will write about it in the next subchapter, devoted to objectivity.
140 Jürgen Habermas, *The Theory of Communicative Action*, vol. 1: *Reason and the Rationalization of Society*, trans. by Thomas McCarthy, Beacon Press, Boston 1984, pp. 1, 3.

can also be rational or irrational: to summarise, all creations (creatures) are investigated by social sciences and feeding them with objects to speak of.[141] Thus, the notion of rationality has an ontological sense, which in sociology means practical (onto-epistemological), in the meaning given to this term by Aristotle when he talked about practical sciences (*praxis*).

Rationality is a fundamental category of social reality and an elementary idea of sociology. This double location of rationality, on the level of objects and on the level of knowledge, engenders complications due to sociology's initial adoption of the scientificity ideal from natural sciences. Rationality appropriated by natural and mathematical sciences had been reduced to procedural rationality. "In the times of the Vienna Circle the place of Reason was already occupied by Science, identified with reason".[142] Rationality, maybe because of the spectacular success of scientific thought embodied in technology, was attributed only to scientific thinking and its technological derivatives. It was an opinion shared not only by philosophers of science or philosophers accepting the scientific outlook, but also representatives of social sciences.[143] Almost simultaneously with the era of triumphant positivism other concepts of rationality emerged, independent from natural sciences, where the idea of rationality is most often identified with the idea of order having neither purely objective determinants (substantial rationality) not purely subjective (procedural rationality).

Max Weber made rationality referring to action the main subject matter of sociology. He devised a typology of rationality correlated with a typology of social actions. Social action is, he says, the main topic of sociology. It differs from behaviour in being intentional, it has a subjective purpose (given by the agent) and it is intersubjective (directed at another

---

141 Habermas, p. 8 and onwards.
142 Edmund Mokrzycki, *Wstęp*, in: *Racjonalność i styl myślenia*, (*Introduction*, in: *Rationality and Thinking Style*), Wydawnictwo IFiS PAN, Warszawa 1992, p. 9.
143 Cf. Edward Evan Evans-Pritchard, *Witchcraft, Oracles and Magic Among the Azande*, Oxford University Press 1976. A critique of that stance was demonstrated by Peter Winch. Cf. Peter Winch, *Understanding a Primitive Society*, "American Philosophical Quarterly" 1964, no. 1, pp. 307-324.

person). [144] Weber demonstrated that rationalisation passing from the sphere of thought to widely understood social life is the main feature of modernity, forging a new social order he calls the "disenchanted world". The principal task of sociology is meant to be understanding these changes. Nevertheless he uses the term rationality in an ambiguous way, possibly hesitating between the technological and praxistic manners of explaining its sense. For him, understanding refers rather to the method than to the social world and interpersonal relations.[145] However, his descendant, Alfred Schütz, already directs his thinking towards everyday lifeworld (here in Husserl's wake) and links the idea of rationality to intersubjectivity (here as Weber's descendant).[146] Recalling William James's theory of notion, he wrote that „our concept has its fringes surrounding a nucleus of its unmodified meaning".[147] The same notion used in contexts of different problems leads to modifying "fringes" around the nucleus, and can possibly even lead to changes within the nucleus. That is why we should distinguish levels referred to by the term of rationality. For example, one of them can be the social world where we naively live and the social world as an object of scientific observation. Rational actions, according to Schütz, are ideal types, not encountered in everyday life. Firstly, ideal types of rationality always refer to problems, ideal types cannot be talked about as such. Secondly, they concern only certain fragments of reality, not the world as such. Therefore the concept of rationality as a key concept also has its fringes and we should remember that each change within the problem (what rationality we speak of, on which level, practice or theory (methodology), or metatheory?) entails a change of notions and types it uses, otherwise we face substantial misunderstandings.

---

144 On rationality in Weber's sociology cf. Stanislav Anderski, *Max Weber's Insights and Errors*, Routledge, London 2010.

145 Cf. Dirk Kaesler, *Max Weber. Eine Einführung in Leben, Werk und Wirkung* (*Max Weber. A Guide to Life, Work and Influences*, Campus Verlag, Frankfurt-New York 2003.

146 Cf. Alfred Schütz, *The Problem of Rationality in Social World*, „Economica" 1943, vol. 10, no. 38, pp. 130-149.

147 Schütz, *The Problem of Rationality in Social World*, p. 133.

The 20th-century sociology largely secures its disciplinary autonomy by abandoning the epistemocentric concept of procedural rationality. This, in many cases, paves the way to the onto-epistemological concept of rationality. Many factors contribute to this metamorphosis.

Although early modern philosophy has appropriated the problem of rationality, its ontological understanding still existed on its fringes. In the so-called practical philosophy: in social philosophy, in political philosophy, later in social sciences, an opposition appeared to "methodologism" (e.g. in Gadamer's hermeneutics), a view identifying the problem of rationality with the problem of rational method.[148] Procedural, methodical rationality is based on the metaphysical separation of the subject and the object of cognition, which is a significant obstacle in a situation where the investigating subject belongs to the subject matter of the investigation.

Another cause can be seen in exhausting the belief in understanding procedural rationality as a repertoire of "ultimate tools", leading to incorrigible, objective truths. The empirical and historically open social process makes sciences, sociology in the first place, open, that is accepting the view that there are no ultimate rules of effective science, that they are mutable, because they have been inscribed in the conditions of their subject matter's mutability.

Defiance of epistemocentrism engenders a situation where the problems of rationality is entangled in a philosophical question reaching the tradition of "hyperrationalism". From Plotinus to Hegel this question was repeatedly asked: can theoretical (scientific) mind, not being a universal mind, but a certain projection of rationality of social orders, produce a transcendental, universal, timeless perspective of critique? This question also includes the enterprise of sociology: whether and how can sociological study step outside and beyond conditions socially determining this study? Can intelligibility of the subject matter of sociology be available to cognitively and ontically limited agents? The question is extremely difficult, because it leads to sociology entangled philosophically: either to post-critical versions of transcendentalism (Karl-Otto Apel, Jürgen Habermas) or to the idea of counter-science (Michel Foucault), which possibly represents

---

148 Cf. Gadamer, *Truth and Method*, pp. 384-405.

the modern version of "emancipative" concept of mind (Theodor Adorno, Hebert Marcuse).

Finally, the most significant issue: in sociology, the problem of rationality is as primordial as the problem of intersubjectivity and inextricably related to intersubjectivity. In the area of social sciences, the question of rationality cannot be asked without the relation to intersubjectivity. Habermas, like Schütz, considers the problem of rationality in relation to intersubjectivity, as a fundamental issue of social sciences. The consequence of the privileged subject/object relation in philosophy of consciousness is the emergence of cognitive-instrumental rationality. Habermas finds this model inadequate and narrow.[149] That is why he proposes a model of communicational rationality. He thought that the appropriate ground for considerations of rationality is provided by social reality, which is the source area where the idea of rationality forms. The basic task of social theory has a reconstructive character and constitutes an answer to the question: how do individuals attach their actions to other individuals' actions? How is coherence of these actions possible? How is communication possible? Rationality correlated with intersubjectivity is a requirement of human actions and thoughts, as long as they refer to other people's thoughts and actions. Conversely, in epistemocentric tradition mono-subjective understanding of an individual and of rationality is the dominant view. That leads to highly speculative constructions in the vein of Leibniz's monadology.

This state of affairs gives rise to a problem unknown in natural sciences. The question arises about specific characteristics of practical/social rationality and sciences' (here: sociology's) ability to capture it adequately. Do social conditions of scientific knowledge production not influence the notion of rationality these sciences use? Since in social sciences, scholars became commonly aware of social context in knowledge production and of its part in social reality (in modern times it concerns mainly scientific knowledge), the question of the relation between rationality governing researchers' professional actions and practical rationality intellectually

---

149 Cf. Habermas, *The Theory of Communicative Action*, pp. 8-42, 273-338.

reproduced by them from actions of social agents, institutions and other similar entities endowed with causal power, has become essential.[150]

So, how should we understand the relation between practical rationality, born and reproduced in the conditions of compulsions and circumstances of action, which do not have the form of intellectual or logical compulsions, and purely cognitive rationality characterising science, identifiable also when compulsions other than those imposed by the cognitive relation are suspended? Is this a relation of opposition or subjugation, or maybe they are complementary? The weight of these questions is exacerbated by the awareness of specific characters and difficulties of investigating objects of social sciences, the awareness that has contributed to social sciences' self-knowledge since early 20th century. Ideas like "humanistic coefficient", concepts like the theory of "social sciences' peculiarity" and many others, are already classical testimonies to recognition of these difficulties. At the same time, they are proposals on how to get out of the trouble in research provoked by what bears the common name of *praxis*. These doubts and problems, unknown on the ground of natural sciences, can assume the form of a question already asked by Edmund Husserl, about the ability of pure reason, "reduced" in its worldly being, to delve into human existence entangled in the "everyday lifeworld" (*Lebenswelt*). The opposition of participation and observation becomes an obstacle in systematically conducted research both in specific investigational situations in the field and in abstract, purely theoretical considerations. It is an obstacle because observation and participation are characterised according to qualifications belonging to utterly different manners of categorisation: whether it is about the trichotomy "theoretical sciences – practical sciences – productive sciences", or about the dichotomy known from post-Cartesian epistemologies (value – fact, subject – object, subjective – objective etc.), these difficulties keep returning in social thought. However, nowadays it is about learning to control these factors rather than only

---

150 Cf. Alfred Schütz, *Common-Sense and Scientific Interpretation of Human Action*, in: Alfred Schütz, *Collected Papers*, vol. I: *The Problem of Social Reality*, ed. Maurice Natanson, Nijhoff, The Hague 1962, pp. 3-47.

recognise them. The condition of making such a step forward is determining the relation between practical and purely cognitive rationality.

Bourdieu pointed out the essential limitations of scientific models using the notion of purely cognitive (scientific) rationality. Against scientific rationality, constituted by the scholastic mind, he pitches practical rationality, that develops and acts in a contingent way, local but dependent on a broad social context.[151] It is an embodiment of action intelligibility, distinct, on the one hand, from intelligibility of purely intellectual acts, and on the other hand, from technological achievements. These are constructed in order to trespass the context in which they have come into being and liberate thought from contingencies of circumstances, goals, history, tradition etc. What distinguishes practical rationality is its autopoietic and interpretative character. Autopoietic character of practical rationality lies in the process of shaping the very agent through activity. Rationality in its autopoietic character is close to the stoic *arete*, virtue, moral bravery, in a sense that stoics gave it, acknowledging identity of *logos* (rationality) of the world and of the human being, moral action. Though, it differs from the stoics' virtue in its historicity and local character. The stoics imposed their cosmopolitan metaphysics on individual morality, demanding of rationality to possess a cosmic dimension. Contrary to that, practical rationality, when shaping subjectivity of action, individualises it and restricts abilities governing choices. Therefore autopoietic action is self-causative and self-creative, it is fulfilled by constant shaping of a kind of moral vigilance towards the self and openness to changes carried by the surrounding world. This aspect of practical rationality is perfectly captured by Bourdieu:

> Habitus is what you have to posit to account for the fact that, without being rational, social agents are reasonable - and this is what makes sociology possible. People are not fools; they are much less bizarre or deluded than we would spontaneously believe precisely because they have internalized, through a protracted and multisided process of conditioning, the objective chances they face. They know how to "read" the future that fits them, which is made for them and for which they are made (by opposition to everything that the expression "this is

---

151 Cf. Bourdieu and Wacquant, *An Invitation to Reflexive Sociology*, pp. 126, 223-234.

not for the likes of us" designates), through practical anticipations that grasp, at the very surface of the present, what unquestionably imposes itself as that which "has" to be done or said (and which will retrospectively appear as the "only" thing to do or say). [...] ("We are empirical", said Leibniz, by which he meant practical, "in three quarters of our actions").[152]

"Objective chances" is an appropriate description of the correlation intelligibility character, and at the same time of confrontation between action and contextual conditions of its success or failure.

In turn, interpretative character of practical rationality reveals in dependence of actions and objects of *autopoiesis* of their past states (*hysteresis*). The point of departure for interpretation, in the sense of an act of practical reason, is always a certain state of affairs, understood as an effect of the dynamics in the relation of a subject with its environment (Bourdieu defines it as a correlation of a "disposition" and a "field") in the form of a "trace" left by an action in the very agent, a modification of the state the agent has been in so far. That trace, modification of a disposition, is subject to interpretation, since its meaning, in order to make further action possible, must retain its dual sense: as an effect of a relation between the environment of others present and others cooperating, but also an effect of changes in its internal states. Reproducing dispositions in an environment altered by actions must reproduce that duality, that is, must lead to constant compulsion of interpretation. Otherwise, activity loses its autopoietic character. Incorporating that trace into a disposition is carried out through interpretation, which never has a purely intellectual character. It is both recognition and modification of the self. Interpretation always has the sense of search and recognition of the boundary between the subjective and the objective, because each action shifts that boundary. It shapes and changes the agent in processes that establish that agent and regulates the agent's reference to the environment by acts brought into reality in activity. This means that it is always situational and unnecessarily with the participation of conscious control, but in a way autopoietically shaped by the agent.

---

152 Bourdieu and Wacquant, *An Invitation to Reflexive Sociology*, pp. 129-130, 131.

The onto-epistemological sense of the interpretational moment of practical rationality depends on the fact that it is a condition of action, as long as every action modifies a subject's disposition: it leaves a cognitive trace of its activity and simultaneously it modifies disposition of cognition. Where epistemological approach to rationality is deemed a privileged perspective, or even the only sensible way of talking about it, the following thesis is tacitly adopted: reaching rationality in the meaning of ontic qualification, like: "rationality of an individual, of an action or an institution" can only be achieved through theoretical knowledge about the individual, the action, the institution. Therefore it is assumed that rationality is not an immanent characteristic of an object, but an effect of intentional projection allowing to capture the manner of their activity.

Bourdieu says that this approach is a typical product of the scholastic mind. The way of thinking subjugated to the scholastic reason leads to imposing rules governing theories on practice. These rules apply a kind of *epoché* to their relation with the subject conducting a scientific investigation. The epistemological privilege of rationality, apart from the disjunction: theory – practice, leads to another one: "»logical absolutism« which claims the right to give the scientific method »logical foundations«" *versus* social or historical constructivism.[153] As a result, adopting epistemological exclusivity in defining the question of science's rationality and projecting its results onto other products of social activities leads to a critique of constructivism, opposed by objectivism. This criticism is armed with the label of relativism, expressing its epistemological sense. Bourdieu, exactly because he adopts an onto-epistemological concept of practice, also criticises the objectivist intellectualism of structuralism.[154] In his opinion, structuralism too easily passes from a model to reality or even takes a model for reality, creating an illusion following a scholastic pattern.

Bourdieu calls a certain view on the place of rules in social life scholastic legalism. Its essence boils down to the idea that practices are executions of

---

153 Cf. Pierre Bourdieu, *Outline of a Theory of Practice*, trans. Richard Nice, University Press, Cambridge 1995, pp. 1-71.

154 In Durkheim's sociology, in de Saussure's linguistics, in Lévi-Strauss's ethnology. Cf. Bourdieu, *Outline of a Theory of Practice*, pp. 22-30.

certain rules.[155] In this view, rules always precede practices. These in turn acquire a social character through executing some general model, pattern, structure. Therefore, rules become hypostases of abstract entities, among them for example "culture", "structures", "social classes" or "production methods". For Bourdieu, a typical case of legalistic thinking is provided by Claude Lévi-Strauss's structural anthropology, where structural models constructed analogically to those devised by linguists (Ferdinand de Saussure, Nicolai Troubetzkoy, Roman Jakobson) are endowed with real, mental being. This model contributes to abandoning naïve ethnocentrism in social sciences, as it allows to disregard the beliefs of culture participants in analyses of indigenous cultures. However, it commits a specific sin. This sin can and should be criticised for producing an intellectual artefact, which is legalistic understanding of social life rules:

> Hence it is not sufficient for anthropology to break with native experience and the native representation of that experience: it has to make a second break and question the presuppositions inherent in the position of an outside observer, who, in his preoccupation with *interpreting* practices, is inclined to introduce into the object the principles of his relation to the object, as is attested by the special importance he assigns to communicative functions (whether in language, myth, or marriage). Knowledge does not merely depend, as an elementary relativism teaches, on the particular standpoint an observer "situated in space and time" takes up on the object. The "knowing subject", as the idealist tradition rightly calls him, inflicts on practice a much more fundamental and pernicious alteration which, being a constituent condition of the cognitive operation, is bound to pass unnoticed: in taking up a point of view on the action, withdrawing from it in order to observe it from above and from a distance, he constitutes practical activity as an *object of observation and analysis*, a *representation*.[156]

The difficulty that legalism provokes in understanding how rules function socially, depends on "utter oblivion of the question about the principle of producing regularities".

Bourdieu's criticism is then "theoretical hypercriticism and metacriticism". He strives to determine the conditions of theoretical control of influence exerted by researchers' social position on the way they objectivise human social behaviours and, consequently, determine the social conditions

---

155 Cf. Bourdieu, *Outline of a Theory of Practice*, p. 27 and next.
156 Bourdieu, *Outline of a Theory of Practice*, p. 2.

enabling separation of the investigating mind from the active subject, the conditions of separation between *episteme* and *praxis*. Thus, it is hypercriticism, as it is an attempt to "objectivise the objectivising" scientific mind. This criticism is directed not only at the form of scientific objectivism, unaware that participation or separation from practices can shape the objectivity of cognition. Bourdieu's criticism is also aimed at another way of theoretical investigation entangled in scholastic mind, which is phenomenological investigation. Although he situates it outside what he calls objectivist cognition, he finds acceptance for the scholastic way of treating practice there. Phenomenological cognition is cognition co-experiencing the social world as given. Therefore, phenomenological cognition explains how the social world may acquire the obviousness of being among people. There is a third way of building a theory, namely praxeological cognition, and that is a tool for the above-mentioned criticism:

> The critical break with objectivist abstraction ensuing from inquiry into the conditions of possibility, and thereby, into the limits of the objective and objectifying standpoint which grasps practices from outside, as a *fait accompli*, instead of constructing their generative principle by situating itself within the very movement of their accomplishment, has no other aim than to make possible a science of the *dialectical* relations between the objective structures to which the objectivist mode of knowledge gives access and the structured dispositions within which those structures are actualized and which tend to reproduce them. This questioning of objectivism is liable to be understood at first as a Rehabilitation of subjectivism and to be merged with the critique that naïve humanism levels at scientific objectification in the name of "lived experience" and the rights of "subjectivity". In reality, the theory of practice and of the practical mode of knowledge inherent in all practice which is the precondition for a rigorous science of practices carries out a new reversal of the problematic which objectivism has to construct in order to constitute the social world as a system of objective relations independent of individual consciousnesses and wills.[157]

The meaning of the notion of a rule in social practice depends on the fact that its specific, so to speak, praxistic sense, is meant to protect social science both from the aberration of objectivism and from one contained in phenomenological cognition. In social life no one has to use the image of the whole to take part in reproduction and production of conditions

---

157 Bourdieu, *Outline of a Theory of Practice*, pp. 3-4.

in which the society lives, in creating orders of culture. Practical rationality comes into being and is reproduced in conditions of compulsions and circumstances of activity and there is no way around it. Practical reason is autochthonic and autonomous: it can be best explained in the conditions where it emerged. It is the strongest expression of rationality's onto-epistemological character.

3. Onto-epistemology of objectivity

Objectivity, like rationality, is a category strongly rooted in theoretical and practical order.

It is universally considered a value both in scientific discourse and in ordinary communication. In popular notion what is objective, is not only important, good and worth attention, but also necessary and it does not allow an alternative. Objectivity plays the role of a connector between thought and reality, between rationality of actions and their results. Similarly in science, objectivity most often passes for undebatable value, the goal of methodology and an indispensable purpose of science, being at the same time the way objects of research exist. It is because objectivity is a category of cognition, as well as the categorial determinacy of being. Hence the trouble with its unequivocal understanding. This "categorial mess" gains significance both in the order of thinking and that of action, especially when objectivity is treated as a category of social sciences. Here, if we set apart certain radical forms of social behaviourism, a scholar inevitably faces a situation whose sociological and philosophical understanding is reflected in Znaniecki's concept of humanistic coefficient. Facts investigated by sociologists or other representatives of social sciences appear to them not as "pure", but as already interpreted by someone else. We can suspect that this interpretation follows multiple paths at the same time, through experience, thinking and activity. In the human world, thus in the world of meanings and values, before a cultural fact gains objective existence, it already exists as someone's thought, someone's intention, someone's experience. The passage from subjective existence to its objective form is fluent and it happens through objectivisation. This corresponds to the specific sensitivity of social sciences, whereas it poses a problem for those who wish to do these sciences in the spirit of epistemocentrism.

Another kind of "categorial mess" is related to the change in the meaning of objectivity that took place after Kant's "Copernican breakthrough" and, consequently, in relation to conceptualisation of objectivity's ontological and epistemological status. After the intellectual revolution launched by Descartes and sanctioned by Kant's criticism, the previous manner of construing knowledge changes completely: from the receptive model to the constructive one. Investigation becomes a subject's activity, whose validity is guaranteed by his/her cognitive powers, that is by the *a priori* forms of sensibility, categories of intellect and ideas of reason. Before modernity cognition was understood as direct seeing[158] or, like in the Middle Ages, as reading.[159] Both channels of cognition, seeing and reading, were complementary. Where reading failed, Platonian seeing, that is "seeing with the soul's eyes", could reach the world's intelligibility. Hence the medieval and Renaissance authority of the Book did not disqualify or replace proper seeing. Cognition-seeing and cognition-reading diverge only in the wake of constructive understanding of cognition. When Johannes Kepler, by investigating the structure of the eye, discovers not only that seeing is anchored in the real world, but also that seeing can be understood as the eye's activity, his contemporary Galileo is ready to ponder the primacy of the Book of the World to the Book of Revelation and observation to reading.[160] The necessity to reconsider the basis the objectivity concept appears when boundaries of studious activity need to be marked, subject it to critique and determine the conditions when it is possible. As long as acquiring knowledge was seen as a receptive process, in which ideas impose themselves on the mind, the problem of objectivity did not exist. It was universally assumed that the moment of intelligibility in study and knowledge resides outside the investigating subject, in the norms of reading,

---

158 Cf. Krzysztof Pomian, *Trzy modele poznania*, (*Three Models of Cognition*) in: *Obecność. Leszkowi Kołakowskiemu w 60 rocznicę urodzin* (*Presence. For Leszek Kołakowski on His 60th Birthday*), „ANEKS", London 1987, pp. 97-98.

159 Cf. Curtius Ernst Robert, *Literatura europejska i łacińskie średniowiecze*, (*European Literature and Latin Middle Ages*), trans. Andrzej Borowski, Universitas, Kraków 1997, pp. 309-357.

160 Cf. Pomian, *Trzy modele poznania*, p. 99.

hence, in superindividual text organisation or in objects themselves, available to investigation thanks to the norms of seeing, as reflecting the order of objective forms. Therefore, the beginning of conceptualising objectivity may be located at the moment when cognition began to be treated as a finite subject's activity.

Lorraine Daston and Peter Galison, science historians, in their book titled *Objectivity*,[161] convincingly argue for the thesis that is hard to reconcile with many still prevalent philosophical views and with colloquial intuition. The thesis follows: objectivity is a value that appeared in science relatively recently. Although the authors do not question the significance of specific aspects of the meaning carried by the notion of objectivity in earlier science, they state that objectivity in the sense known from today's scientific discussions and practices, is a value born in the process encompassing merely the second half of the 19th century and the 20th. Changes taking place nowadays, especially those which link objectivity as a value of knowledge to human ability to objectivise, contribute to further modifications of this category. According to Daston and Galison, the key moment in the history of the category of objectivity is the second half of the 19th century, since then in natural sciences a new terminological usus ("objective") emerges and it comes to mean what it means now.

And what was it like before? Why did radical changes take place in using the notion of objectivity? In all modern European languages, the word "objective" was derived from the adjectival or adverbial Latin form *obiectivus, obiective*.[162] These terms always occurred in two pairs of antonyms: *obiectivus – subiectivus* and *obiective – subiective*. In the language of philosophy they appear thanks to the 14th-century thinkers: Duns Scotus and William of Ockham, who used the term *esse obiectivum* construed "as that which exists only through an act of investigating, as an intentional being", that is, as existence proper to knowable content.[163] On the other hand, *subiective* concerned things in themselves. So, these

---

161 Cf. Lorraine Daston, Peter Galison, *Objectivity*, Zone Books, New York 2007 and Lorraine Daston, Elizabeth Lundbeck, *Histories of Scientific Observation*, The University of Chicago Press, Chicago, London 2011.
162 Cf. Daston, Galison, *Objectivity*, p. 29.
163 Cf. Daston, Galison, *Objectivity*, p. 29 and next.

terms were used in exactly reverse meanings to the ones we use today: the adjective "objective" referred to things as they are given to consciousness, and "subjective" described things as such, things in themselves, as we would say nowadays. Thus, "subjective" meant as much as "referring to an object", while "objective" referred to a mental image of or critical take on that object. E. Chambers's *Universal Dictionary of Arts and Sciences*, published in 1728, states: „Hence a thing is said to *exist* OBJECTIVELY, *objectivé*, when it exists no otherwise than in being known; or in being an Object of the Mind".[164] Throughout the 17th and 18th centuries the pair: *subiective – obiective* was understood by metaphysicians and logicians as technical terms, according to such, now only historic, sense. The fundamental change, as the authors of *Objectivity* say, is related to the breakthrough in philosophy achieved by Kant. The latter gives this couple of terms (objective – subjective) a reversed, specific meaning motivated by the "Copernican revolution". In his philosophy objectivity is object-related validity (*objektive Gültigkeit*). It refers not to the existence of objects external to the mind, which are what they are in themselves (*Gegenstände*), but to forms of sensibility, which are conditions of experience. In consequence, in Kant's philosophy the boundary between the objective and the subjective separates the universal and necessary from the particular and casual for the investigating mind, not between the world and the mind.[165] On the one hand, Kant reverses meanings known from the repertoire of scholastic thought, on the other he shifts the boundary between them. What is universal in the mind by projection of its forms on experience, is at the same time objective in a representation, that is, objectively valid, constitutive for the object. Conversely, what is particular or casual in the representation, must be such in the mind, unnecessary. Kant referred objectivity to relation with objects, but he conceived the conditions of that as dependent on what is universal in the mind. In other words, the conditions of what is object-related (hence, what exists *subiective* in the scholastic sense), are located for Kant in the mind, not in things. This way revolutionary reversal of meanings occurred.

---

164 I quote from Daston, Galison, *Objectivity*, p. 29.
165 Cf. Daston, Galison, *Objectivity*, p. 30.

Natural sciences adopted the idea contained in Kant's innovation by
an interpretation that could be called "experimental": objectivity is what
allows to extract an object from experience. It is mainly experiment that
extracts the object of knowledge from worldly involvements, especially
the extra-cognitive ones. Thus the term "objective" immediately gained
ambivalence known also from the modern usus: it has come to mean an
object's existence independent from a subject, agent (*subiectum*) and its
subjective, that is, particular, contents of experience, or a description of
unbiased character of an agent's investigational efforts, neutralising the
influence of the particular and experiential. The terminological mess
lasted until the end of the 1850s. In 1817 Samuel Taylor Coleridge could
then write:

> „Now the sum of all that is merely OBJECTIVE, we will henceforth call NA-
> TURE, confining the term to its passive and material sense, as comprising all the
> phaenomena by which its existence is made known to us. On the other hand the
> sum of all that is SUBJECTIVE, we may comprehend in the name of the SELF or
> INTELLIGENCE. Both conceptions are in necessary antithesis."[166]

On the one hand, the 1820s and 1830s brought definitions close to the
modern understanding: objectivity characterises cognition of an external
object and subjectivity is immanence and in opposition to objectivity. On
the other hand, until the 1860s the meaning of the word *obiective* attributed to Kant appears as a novelty in French dictionaries.[167]

Natural sciences absorbed the concepts of subjectivity and objectivity
with an additional modification, significant in relation to the Kantian
meaning, concerning assessment of cognitive abilities of real agents. The
process of discovering a subject (agent) as a condition of gaining knowledge had already begun in early 17th century, and Kant's philosophy was
its culmination. In the area of natural sciences, it gained the sense of discovering an obstacle to knowledge. These sciences (e.g. physiology and
medicine) discovered for themselves not as much a universal and transcendental subject (such as in Kant's epistemology), as such an agent that could
be an object of their research, that is, real, carnal and in this carnality

---

166 I quote from Daston, Galison, *Objectivity*, p. 30.
167 Cf. Daston, Galison, *Objectivity*, p. 31.

bound to commit errors, a possible obstacle for knowledge.[168] That is why the notion of objectivity understood as unbiasedness, neutrality, gains weight wherever imperfection of knowledge must be laid on the very investigating agent. It is entangled in the bias proper to its cultural environment, unbounded by the laboratory rigour, not universal enough in the norms of modern intellectual culture. Objectivity construed this way is becoming a highly regarded value with the growing awareness of the role played by all factors in the cognitive process that cannot be normalised in a situation of observation or experiment, that is, procedurally or technologically. Then an obstacle emerges impeding correct functioning of the mind's ability to adequately capture objects, an ability whose effectiveness depends on suppression of all particularities of subjectivity. This obstacle gets noticed and becomes an object of investigative and corrective efforts in scientific practice. In other words, still, in research practice and later also in epistemological thought on sciences, a new sort of epistemological obstacle appears as a result of these changes: the researcher's particular subjectivity. It is seen in opposition to cognitive powers of Scientific Reason, universal in their abilities, and in opposition to the compulsions of tradition. This way "objectivity" becomes a concept spliced with two other concepts: "rationality" and "intersubjectivity". What is "objective", acquires such modern definitions that it can be rationalised in different ways (cognitively and extra-cognitively, e.g. technologically) but also what is "objective", becomes a basis of a modern requirement from knowledge, that of universal intelligibility. In practice, including scientific practice, this means the necessity to participate in communities of scholars – a requirement of intersubjectivity.

---

168 Disbelief and distrust to individual (also one's own) results of investigation rouses autocriticism in a human being: "Can I see it well? Isn't it an illusion? Do I recognise it correctly? Does such a phenomenon really exist?" The criterion verifying and evaluating knowledge must be located outside the individual intellect: either in universal rationality or in confirmations performed by other entities or the whole community. These social references and involvement of communication, including controversy, in the process of determining the status of a specific discovery shift the meaning of "objectivity" closer to "intersubjectivity".

The scientific revolution, which occurred in the 16th and 17th centuries, sparked the process of radical change of notions crucial to modern understanding of knowledge. Above all, these include experience, subject, object. Direct experience, linking the world of scholars' community with their cultural environment, gets replaced by the notion of experience construed as it has shaped its content in situations of experiments, technically constructed observation and mediated or in a situation of measurement.[169] Experience produced technologically in observatories and laboratories separated the agent of scientific study from colloquial culture (dogmatically petrified). Using technology to cognitive ends imposed on the investigating agent specific conditions of cognition, unknown in that culture, epistemically alien, hence unintelligible and redundant.[170] Practical difficulties or attempts at retaining identical conditions of experiments revealed the part played by a researcher as a factor disrupting the course of a natural phenomenon with his/her activity, and they led to considering a real agent an obstacle to knowledge.

Compensating that flaw, technology paved an important way of overcoming the constraints of an agent's cognitive finiteness. To produce objective knowledge, an investigator must subsume to a regime that forces to apply technology in investigation. Since technology in science is nothing else than theory brought into life, technologically intermediated experience, armed with laboratory equipment, confronts the "investigated thing" with the "investigating thing" and gives a chance to eliminate possible

169 Religious doctrine and scholastic philosophy made scholars utterly dependent on social and institutional criteria of value of knowledge. Defiance and rebellion against that manifested in giving preference to other criteria, that is, individualised and, in intention, culturally neutral. In philosophy of early modern rationalism and empiricism the social character of knowledge was reduced as far as possible and transformed into a hybrid techno-rational objectivisation which an experiment is.

170 The cognitive and practical success of experiment, as a fact construed in an early modern way, made technological procedures the main source of knowledge. The social character of the individualist revolt in the concept of knowledge changed history, but paradoxically, eliminated an individual agent from influence on knowledge. It enforced obedience to rational and technological procedures, which are rather methodological conformism than trust in individual creativity.

differences of human sensitivities, involved in the process of acquiring knowledge. An effect obtained this way is a natural phenomenon, correct and repeatable, guaranteed by honesty of the procedure based on trust in intelligibility embodied in a scientific instrument.

This understanding of functions performed by various forms of disciplining compulsion, which investigating agents should be subject to, is contributed to by the process of adapting Kant's philosophy to sciences. It is especially visible in the change that occurred in assessment of representations in scientific (natural) atlases in the 19th century.[171] Around 1860, publishers of atlases of nature started to look for perfect, accurate, objective in the sense of unbiasedness, way of representing specimens of nature. They sought techniques that discipline perception and leave as little room as possible for subjective, prone to fleeting enchantment, biased impression. Representation of a concrete object becomes valued, as opposed to universal or ideal type, as it has been before. Consequently, a change occurred in assessment of the value of images in these atlases. Before they had been esteemed when artists and scientists who had created them, had managed to capture objective, typical, if not universal, characteristics of these objects: fish, butterflies, ferns. An image had been valuable knowledge-wise, because it represented not a concrete object, but a species; it had been executed according to objectivity understood in the Kantian way, in its universality. In the practice of preparing atlases the key role was played by coincidence of two couples of concepts: subjective – objective and particular – universal. Around 1860 it was discovered, as Daston and Galison claim, that the very investigating subject can be an obstacle due to the subject's particularity and a quest began for eliminating it.[172] This change took place in the scientific culture of publishers and users of natural atlases and it was supported in a broader context when the conviction spread of opposing functions of artistic and scientific representations. The former have an expressive function in relation to the object of creation (subjectivity is their primary property and function),

171 Cf. Daston, Galison, *Objectivity*, pp. 34-35.
172 Cf. Daston, Galison, *Objectivity*, p. 35.

whereas the latter have a function of objectivising experience concerning the object of representation.

An antecedent confirming the above-mentioned authors' diagnoses may be seen in Ludwik Fleck's remark on drawings of a uterus in 17th-century anatomical atlases, which did not reflect its true appearance, were not "correct" or "compliant with reality". They were imaginations shaped by now past views on what is cognitively valuable, and what Fleck himself describes with terms that would not encourage contemporary naturalists' trust: „All had been touched up in appearance, and were schematically, almost symbolically, true to theory but not to nature."[173]

Growth of knowledge achieved under the supervision of modern "objectivity" shows contrast between a natural subject (a subject of natural cognitive powers) and a subject given with participation of cognition technology. Standardisation and universalisation of cognitive technology engenders conditions of critique aimed at a scientific self, an agent performing scientific activities. It becomes a significant factor of epistemological auto-pedagogy conducted by agents of research and their calibration. In this context objectivity can be understood as a consequence of these changes in scientific investigation, a result of discovering the contrast between a natural subject and an extended one. This process began at the turn of the 17th century and it fully fledged in the second half of the 19th century.

What does investigation gain and what does it lose when we radically transform it in the technological extension of cognition? What are the results of the historic transformation of direct experience into "communication with an object" thanks to instruments of research and measurement, which are onto-epistemic constructions?[174]

---

173 Fleck, *Genesis and Development of a Scientific Fact*, p. 33.
174 In the olden days, a doctor taking patients' temperature had to touch them, then analyse (and possibly also reflect on) subjective experience and assess it according to past experience. Nowadays a thermometer is a medium thanks to which the patient is touched not by a "subject", but by "matter" and it is the latter that presents the result of an "interaction" of a thermometer with the patient. The result of that interaction is given by a number, being an element of language and "saying" what the objective state of affairs is like. Thus we abandon subjective impressions, but we gain the desired passionless objectivity.

Technology, prominent in science since the 17th century, creates a yawning gap between direct experience, which everyone participates in due to natural constitution, and intermediated experience, technologically extended. This way it differentiates and specialises cognition, making it unavailable to "profane souls" unfamiliar to practices of discipline allowing for its effective use to acquire knowledge. The difference between natural and technologically disciplined cognitive powers started to play a growing role along with the development of the symbiotic correlation of sciences and technology. Consequently, natural cognitive powers began to be treated as limited and attributed lesser investigative effectiveness, not highly efficient in science.[175] Objectivity understood as unbiasedness is founded on the regulatory role of technology that standardises the cognitive process, and procedures based on it, intermediating even the most elementary acts of cognition. This concept of objectivity is used in natural sciences.

Another significant factor making the notion of objectivity a fundamental category of knowledge is the social factor, especially concerning the scholars' community. We are talking here about the process of autonomising the very institutions of science and specialisation of scientific knowledge inscribed in it.[176] In the 19th century this process accelerated, beginning with reforms undertaken by Humboldt brothers (Wilhelm and Alexander) in Germany, and finishing with reforms of French science in the 1870s, which subjugated universities to state authority.

Objectivity understood as unbiasedness (*versus* taking sides) plays an essential role in case of science's institutional autonomy. It is about state guarantees of scholars' unbiasedness and the authority of scientific institutions that it forges, supported by social mechanisms of intellectual

---

An instrument of measure and examination interacts (on entry) as matter with matter, and on exit it displays an epistemic message.

175 Cf. Pomian, *Trzy modele poznania*. The cost of this change is shortage of "empirical sense", for example in physics characteristics and properties of elementary particles are represented exclusively by numbers. We investigate objectively and precisely, but we do not know "what".

176 On this subject cf. Amsterdamski, *The Institutionalization and Professionalization of Scientific Research*, in: *Between History and Method*, pp. 65-78.

and institutional culture and critique. This way two senses of objectivity could be merged into one notion: as object-oriented validity and an agent's unbiasedness. Both were, so to speak, appropriated by the community of scholars and this appropriation gained a social sanction. Linking these two ways of understanding objectivity: as unbiasedness and as object-oriented validity, depends on identifying an unprejudiced view with adequate seeing of things in themselves. In consequence, in scientific practice the following viewpoint is beginning to dominate: it is enough to subject an object of investigation to technological and logical regimes of unbiasedness to achieve objectivity, along with increment of knowledge protected by the objective validity of knowledge. Social conditions, technological and intellectual practices of this kind can from now on be fulfilled only by an autonomous scientific institution, giving a researcher the possibility to studiously explore the world in the spirit of the investigator's (i.e. unbiasedly) and the investigated thing's objectiveness (that is, true to reality).

Even at the first glance, however, it is clearly visible that objectivity construed this way has different meanings in natural and social sciences, respectively. It is because of different social and epistemic backgrounds of these sciences.

In case of social sciences, this background is practical, and not technological. In this case the opposition between *praxis* and *techne*, so significant in antiquity, and abolished in modern natural sciences, is again revived and marks a boundary between important factors of social context in natural and social sciences. What is more, the social entanglement of knowledge in social sciences (marked with associations "separation – autonomy", "involvement – subjugation") has a different sense than in natural sciences. The case of social sciences' practical functions in politics is instructive. Therefore, we must accept consequences of the fact that objectivity as unbiasedness and object-oriented validity is not a result of research intermediation through technology. Thus, knowledge in social sciences must remain on a relatively unspecialised level for the lack of the differentiating factor provided in technology. The function standardising objectivity (in the meaning of unbiasedness and object-oriented validity) is performed not by objectivised technology establishing the regime of method, but the researcher's subjectively and practically (that is, in action) attained knowledge separating, within certain limits and not without a hindrance, scientifically qualified knowledge from colloquial knowledge. Experience in its cognitive functions depends here on confronting the "investigated subject", that is, the object, with the "investigating subject", that is, the researcher. This inevitably heightens the risk of subjective factors affecting the results. The notion of objectivity shaped in natural sciences' practices since mid-19th century is therefore largely useless.

The mentioned risk is reduced through "objectification" of the investigated entity with the use of symbolic practices whose ultimate source is the researcher's culture. That it is a real process of objectivising experience is attested to by two relations of a researcher extremely devoted to objectivity and also very experienced in the field:

> Every time he is in the field, the ethnologist finds himself open to a world where everything is foreign and often hostile to him. He has only his self still at his disposal, enabling him to survive and to pursue his research. But it is a self physically and morally battered by weariness, hunger, discomfort, the shock to acquired habits, the sudden appearance of unsuspected prejudices. It is a self which, in this strange conjuncture, is crippled and maimed by all the blows of a personal history responsible at the outset for his vocation, but which will affect its future course. Hence, in ethnographic experience the observer apprehends himself as his own instrument of observation. Clearly, he must learn to know himself, to obtain, from a *self* who reveals himself as *another* to the *I* who uses him, an evaluation which will become an integral part of the observation of other selves. Every ethnographic career finds its principle in "confessions", written or untold.[177]

The researcher's objectivism is revealed in his critical stance, that Lévi-Strauss calls a confession. In practising it he approaches the status of an extended subject, although not extended technologically, but practically. Being "his own instrument of observation" is a result of a stance objectivising his own self only in exceptional, described by Lévi-Strauss, conditions. Extracting the cognitive sense from them, or practising this torment of self-discipline for the purpose of knowledge, is related to possibility of including its results in the arsenal of research instruments, "observation of other selves". Hence the extraordinary position of ethnology: in an evident way it shows a certain kind of objectivising research practice, known by all social sciences:

---

177 Claude Lévi-Strauss, *Structural Anthropology* vol. II, trans. Monique Layton, Basic Books, Inc., Publishers, New York 1975, pp. 35-36.

The prominent place of ethnography in the sciences of man, which explains the role it already plays in some countries, under the name of social and cultural anthropology, as inspirer of a new humanism, derives from the fact that it offers this unlimited process of objectification of the subject, which is so difficult for the individual to effect; and offers it in a concrete, experimental form. The thousands of societies which exist or have existed on the earth's surface are human, and on that basis we share in them in a subjective way; we could have been born into them, and so we can seek to understand them as if we were. But at the same time, all of them taken together (as compared to any one of them on its own) attest to the subject's capacity to objectify himself in practically unlimited proportions, since the society which is the reference group, which constitutes only a tiny fraction of the given, is itself always exposed to being subdivided into two different societies, one of which promptly joins the enormous mass of that which, for the other one, has and always will have the status of object; and so it goes on indefinitely. Any society different from our own has the status of object; any group of our own society, other than the group we come from ourselves, is an object; and even every custom of our own group to which we do not adhere. That limitless series of objects constitutes, in ethnography, the Object, and is something that the individual subject would have to pull painfully away from himself, if the diversity of mores and customs did not present him with a prior fragmenting. But never could the historical and geographical closing of gaps induce him to forget (at the risk of annihilating the results of his efforts) that all those objects proceed from him, and that the most objectively conducted analysis of them could not fail to reintegrate them inside the analyst's subjectivity.[178]

We deal here with the practical and intellectual process of objectivising simultaneously the object and the subject, that is, the process of acquiring by the investigating subject the special disposition of distancing from himself/herself, correlated with extended cognitive sensitivity to another self. The meaning of this process can be most easily recognised in ethnological practice exactly because symbolic means applied in analysis and those being an object objectivised in it, are separated from each other before the researcher starts the investigation, and differences between them are visible to the naked eye. At the same time this process, to a degree required by conditions of the research's effectivity, is characteristic to each practice where cognitive motivation participates, aimed at another self.

178 Claude Lévi-Strauss, *Introduction of the Work of Marcel Mauss*, trans. Felicity Baker, Routledge and Kegan Paul, London 1987, pp. 32-33.

That is why the objectivising function of institutional autonomy is different in natural sciences and in social sciences. Objectivity as an effect of critique of a natural subject's cognitive powers, in social sciences becomes a distinctive feature of two kinds of knowledge: colloquial (involved) and scientific (neutral). The difference in relation to the form of institutional autonomy in natural sciences appears in social sciences due to the fact that the latter's institutional autonomy does not separate them from a social process, it only changes forms of engaging knowledge in it, with respect to a scholar's social situation compared to an ordinary participant of a social process. Scholars and scientific institutions take part in control of knowledge production not by technology, but by practical forms of controlling results of their activities, by political tests of their credibility and the credibility of applied symbolic research apparatus.

In this context, an important question emerges: where does the difficulty of linking these two meanings of objectivity lie, i.e. understood as unbiasedness and as object-oriented validity, just as it is in natural sciences?

In natural sciences acknowledging that a real subject, as particular, becomes an obstacle to investigation rather than a condition of conducting it, as well as objectivity as unbiasedness and object-oriented validity was contemporaneous to the rise of empirical sciences of man, like sociology. These sciences, following natural sciences, interpret objectivity in two ways at the same time: as unbiasedness guaranteed by the method and the researcher's appropriate (neutral, uninvolved) conduct, and also the result of that conduct, a certain property of knowledge allowing to capture the object.

Studying social facts like things (Durkheim) and studying free from evaluation (Weber) are goals of sociologies following this path. On the other hand, the connection between an agent's cognitive bias and the object-oriented character of investigation, interpreted in the spirit of philosophical (Kantian) traditions, yields a standpoint called constructivism as the basic research stance of sociology. That is why since the beginning in the area of sociology two extremely different projects of social research can be distinguished: one conducted in the name of objectivity (these include sociological theories, starting from Comte, but also Durkheim's sociology of social facts and Weber's sociology free from evaluation), and the other in the name of subjectivity, formed under the influence of transcendentalist

traditions, in the wake of Kant and Husserl, which may be called constructivism (e.g. Schütz's sociology).

The opposition "objectivity – subjectivity", understood statically and
restricted to cognitive issues, has dominated in sociological research
since the rise of sociology as a discipline. Moreover, since the disciplinary
beginnings of sociology, objectivity has been understood as a synonym
and a condition of scientificity.

That is why questions concerning objectivity emerge most often in the
context of sociology's research methods and a result of research process in
the form of a description, a theory or a statement. Sociology faces a difficult, if at all possible, choice between objectivism depending on unbiasedness, but achieved at the cost of giving up attempts to investigate the social
world as it is, including what it is like for this world's inhabitants (for
them, actions and their products are "social facts"), and subjectivism or
constructivism, which reconstructs social orders as emanations of purely
symbolic acts (of all intersubjectivity it only examines communication, as
long as that leads to consent on validation of the world's practical aspect
in existence).

In the first case, we have to do with objectivity understood as unbiasedness, independence, distance, disinvolvement, which in practical order
means being an outsider.[179] It is then about objectivity of investigative
approach. In the second case to have an objective method would mean
to have a method making knowledge of participants in social practices
prone to critique and at the same time sensitive to unobvious facts. In
consequence, the method would be able to objectivise what in practice is
only available in direct experience and activity. An objective method is
supposed to guarantee objective conclusions, hence such that can capture,
portray an object as it truly is, and not as it is seen by a "prejudiced" researcher or member of the society separated from its practices by goals,
tools, practices there unknown and unnecessary (who needs a reconstruction of the social order in Chinese jump rope?). In other words still, an

---

179 The position of scientists-outsiders in their own societies are well portrayed in
two ethnologists' texts: Malinowski's *A Diary in the Strict Sense of the Term*
and Lévi-Strauss's *Tristes Tropiques*.

objective method is one allowing for rational criticism and leads to rational conclusions.

Nevertheless, the above interpretations, starting from the static view of the relation between the objective and the subjective, lead to many difficulties. Objectivity construed as a researcher's unbiased stance, leads to difficulties at the level of understanding links between practice and theory. Disinvolvement at the level of social practice is social indifference leading to anomy. Will an alienated researcher notice essential social phenomena and be a participant of social life able to understand it? On the other hand, can a sociologist avoid socio-cultural entanglements, step beyond them, leave emotions outside, do the same with attitudes, preconceptions, the knowledge proper to a participant and observer of social life? Ready to perform an *epoche* of sorts, does she or he not reduce the object of research and even the researcher as the agent?

A sociologist as a researcher must be an outsider and an insider at the same time, which was perfectly understood by Znaniecki, when he formulated the principle of humanistic coefficient and introduced the autobiographical method to sociology. For him, "objective" meant repeatedly reproduced in course of experience and activity, and belonging to a system of objects. "Objective" does not mean "independent from the investigating subject", but breaking free from it by perpetuating its meaning (continuously expanding), therefore existing as a value. Objectivity, in the sense of adequacy to the object, means dependent on agents, as reality and objectivity of an object depend exactly on multiplicity of experience related to that object, acting with it and on it by as great a number of agents as possible. Thus, contrary to Husserl, "burdened" with the naturalist notion of experience, Znaniecki is not troubled by the world's intersubjectivity.[180]

180 Cf. Florian Znaniecki, *Cultural Reality*, The University Chicago Press, Chicago, Illinois 1919, pp. 40-48. An interesting approach to the issue of objectivity in social sciences is Norbert Elias's, expressed in the work *Involvement and Detachment*, where he introduces socially derived modifications of the notion of objectivity in the form of the terms "involvement" and "detachment". Cf. Norbert Elias, *Involvement and Detachment*, University College Dublin Press, Dublin 2007. See also, Mariola Kuszyk-Bytniewska, *Zaangażowanie a neutralność – o trudnościach stosowania pojęcia obiektywności w naukach społecznych. Onto-epistemologiczna recepcja socjologii N. Eliasa (Involvement*

For him, objectivisation is bringing into reality the structures of activity that at the outset never have a purely subjective or purely objective character. Objectivity is the movement of thought, cognitive insight into an object, which is made possible thanks to the process of objectivising content being material of action, a social process in its nature. Therefore, objectivity understood as a characteristic of investigation is a specific product of objectivisation, an effect of practical availability of certain content, whose experience, thinking and activity enforce a relatively durable form of an object, enabling co-operation and communication. Both, objectivity and objectivisation, construed as part of the cultural process, take part in shaping the human world, concrete reality, as it is called by Znaniecki. The category of action is crucial. Not taking it into account, without involvement in conceptualising objectivity of the intersubjective social world and culture, "objectivity" becomes a category impoverished in its meaning. It is proven both by the history of concepts seeking the "bridge" between being and thought, and by those indicating its inexistence. Znaniecki's philosophy of culture, questioning radical divisions into "objective *vs* subjective" is a good example of awareness of this situation. This philosophy opens science to cultural facts, to meanings and values which "are always somebody's, never nobody's". By ordering reality practically and theoretically (science) we make not only distinctions, but we also mark separating boundaries: objective – subjective, valid and general – relative and particular etc. We do it for formal and logical reasons, as well as methodological ones, as in science. We also do it for social reasons, often casual ones, which solve certain significant issues, of much practical weight. Reality is not only the world available to consciousness in cognition (not as a whole, but aspect-wise), it is also a result and process of human activity. That is why an important problem concerning being and knowing in social sciences must be seen in various forms of intersubjectivity, necessary for the emergence of interactional order, where not as much products of

and Detachment. How to Understand the Inter-Subjectivity of the Social World and the Objectivity of Social Sciences? The Onto-Epistemological Reception of N. Elias' Sociology), „Roczniki Historii Socjologii" 2013, vol. 3, pp. 61-81.

technology are objectivised, as results of practice, creations of human existence environment.

4. Onto-epistemology of intersubjectivity

I understand the category of intersubjectivity as primary both in relation
to subjectivity and to objectivity, as a condition of the society's existence.
Individuals communicate, co-operate and sometimes fight, this way creating a common world of meanings and values: in dialogue, in activities
undertaken together, in competition and in struggle with others. This is
how similarity to others shapes a person's social identity and individual
identity is shaped by how that person differs from others. Intersubjectivity
is forging axionormative orders, but also sharing them. Firstly, they constitute a condition and a result of activity, and only as a consequence they
involve consciousness. This understanding of intersubjectivity makes this
category capable of describing a person's ontic-epistemic relations with
reality.

On the one hand, the philosophical take on intersubjectivity counts
among typical conceptualisations of modern thought. It is related to
questions of how the sense of a person's existence in the world can be
reconciled with the issue of validating his or her self-awareness. How can
a human being be captured by science, that is, empirically, and yet have
the status given by philosophy, the status of *ego cogito*, the *fundamentum
inconcussum* of knowledge. On the other hand, though, this problem
does not fit into the framework of early modern philosophy. Although
it is early modern philosophy that provokes this whole issue, it does not
provide any means to articulate it unequivocally, let alone any solutions.
That is why the problem bears signs of paradox, especially confronted
with scientific and common-sense thought. This is because in thinking of
human self-awareness this philosophy is driven mainly by the Cartesian
metaphysics of cognition. By this I mean the approach to cognition and
knowledge which requires distinguishing two poles of the cognitive relation along with the assumption of their utter heteronomy, irreducible
existential definitions of the subject and the object, like *res cogitans* and
res extensa. This twofold relation makes up a kind of dipole, a bipolar,
heteronomous manifold consisting of elements correlated with cognition

and nothing else. As a result, until Kant this philosophy had lacked reflection on the relation between the transcendental self and the empirical self, as well as the relation between the self construed in investigative mode of its pertinence to the world to the self existentially excluded from that world. Moreover, the conceptualisation of intersubjectivity requires something else still, "squeezing", so to speak, a third element into that "inter" ("between"), adopting the role of an object and a subject at the same time. It is a subject and an object of experience and activity, communication and fight, close and the most alien, in one word: OTHER.

Stanisław Judycki points at three fundamental contexts of conceptualising intersubjectivity in philosophy: 1) the issue of existence of other subjects (in relation to German idealism), i.e. the so-called problem of *alter ego*, the problem of acknowledging another self as an experiencing one; (2) the discussion on conditions of scientific sentences' acceptability (in neopositivism and partially analytic philosophy; (3) in relation to problems of language (Wittgenstein's argument for impossibility of constructing a private language).[181] It is worth adding a fourth formula here, (4) Edmund Husserl's, who asks how to avoid "transcendental solipsism" in view of this problem: how the mono-subjectively given world may be at the same time a world, in its existence correlative to *ego cogito*, common for everyone. All these formulas are variants of a question arisen from the Cartesian metaphysics of cognition, that is, intellectual derivates of establishing the sense of all cognition on the irreducible duality of *ego cogito* and the world, utterly different in nature.

For quite a long time these issues functioned in the shadows, as not fully determined concepts. Finally, due to repetitions and radicalisations of the Cartesian motif of criticism in Kant's and Hegel's philosophy, followed by Husserl in the 20th century, it has been promoted to a role of a fundamental philosophical problem. Since practical philosophy still construed in Aristotelian spirit yielded to a theoretical conceptualisation of human existence, expressed in postulates of humanist and social sciences'

---

181 Cf. Stanisław Judycki, *Intersubiektywność (Intersubjectivity)*, in: *Powszechna Encyklopedia Filozofii (General Encyclopaedia of Philosophy)*, vol. 4, Polskie Towarzystwo Tomasza z Akwinu, Lublin 2003, pp. 893-894.

autonomy, problems of the "transcendental solipsism" kind have motivated a significant part of philosophy's critical potential. Acknowledging
the being of a self other than a pondering, meditating one, has become a
philosophical "puzzle" that the whole idea of Husserl's phenomenology
stumbles upon. It was already visible in *Méditations Cartesiennes*, and
later in *The Crisis of the European Sciences*. If we add, unknown to Kant
and his predecessors, existential, critical to Descartes, problematisations of
ego cogito (Heidegger, Sartre) and questions of social sciences, we see that
in the 20th century the problem of intersubjectivity propelled investigation
in extensive areas of philosophical and scientific thought. These topics appear in diverse critical philosophies, which either assume the form of analytics of being, concerning human existence radically distinguished in the
world (e.g. the form of Heidegger's concept of "existentials"), or, to the
contrary, they treat on social orders and they see the fundamental category
of social being and human existence in the notion of intersubjectivity. The
latter paradigm of thinking is nowadays continued by Jürgen Habermas's
critical philosophy, linking epistemological and transcendental questions
with the issues of emancipation. In this context, we can recall the influence
exerted by Mead's conceptualisation of the problem. He departs from the
pragmatical theory of action, from cooperative understanding of action
seen as "practical intersubjectivity" in order to answer the question how
a mono-subjective self is possible, an "I" operating an objective "me".
These are not at all phenomenological analyses of consciousness depth,
as Husserl's, but a search for a possibly wide horizon of references for the
self.[182]

   In a retrospective glance, Marek J. Siemek claims that the "principle of
individual experience", dominant in Western intellectual culture, is now
construed "as a socially and historically shaped creation of primordially
communicational intersubjectivity, which lies at the base of the very process of socialisation"[183] and it is not even a 20th-century discovery (Wittgenstein and analytic philosophy, Heidegger and hermeneutics, French

---

182 Cf. Georg Herbert Mead, *Mind, Self, and Society. From The Standpoint of a
    Social Behaviorist*, the University of Chicago Press, Chicago and London 1972.
183 Marek J. Siemek, *Hegel i filozofia (Hegel and Philosophy)*, Oficyna Naukowa,
    Warszawa 1988, p. 174.

structuralism). According to Siemek, the sources of placing transcendental intersubjectivity at the base of human communication, culture and reasoning must be sought in analyses of German idealism. For him, the first thinker to recognise the dialogical (hence communicational) structure of intersubjectivity was not Hegel, but Fichte. The Fichtean model of intersubjectivity as mutuality is founded on affirmation of free agents' dialogue. Here communicational intersubjectivity is not a consequence, but the primary premise of thoughtful freedom and individuality. Intersubjectivity is based on understanding, on exchange, on "call and response", on talking and listening. The basic dimension of intersubjectivity seen this way is coordination (of actions, purposes, meanings etc.),[184] whereas the Hegelian model of intersubjectivity is a monological model, "rationality based on dominance", on "struggle for life", which, for Hegel, is a source of primary social bonds. "Struggle for acknowledgement" is the source, and simultaneously the way of achieving intersubjectivity. It is only in fight that another subjectivity gets recognised as subjectivity, as well as an individual's subjectivity becomes established as the "self". The fundamental aspect of so construed intersubjectivity is then subordination: of phenomena, subjects, actions etc.[185]

This kind of dualism in fulfilment forms of intersubjectivity (coordination *versus* subordination) permeates modern thought and shows directions of its conceptualisation. The category of subordination, by intellectual debts mainly to Kant, determines the point of view of epistemology as central and promising a solution to the problem: all orders of representations, harmonies of convictions and unanimities of meanings meet in internal compulsions of *a priori* universal cognitive powers. It is the mono-subjective individual that is endowed with the role of a foundation for the order of representations, and its function is to subordinate the diversity of experience to an intelligible form of cognition. This is the sense of the term "cognitive power". On the other hand, the category of coordination establishes the central point of view of those philosophies and social sciences which treat mono-subjective individuality as a derivative

---

184 Cf. Siemek, *Hegel i filozofia*, pp. 174-186.
185 Cf. Siemek, *Hegel i filozofia*, pp. 186-194.

effect of clashing social forces. In this view, the solution to the problem of intersubjectivity depends on answering the question: how all individual actions meet in practical orders, or axionormative orders, in a way that can constitute the mono-subjective individuality as able to participate in those orders.

Modern thinking is characterised by ambivalence concerning recognition of one of these visions as fundamental. It is clearly visible in mutually remote philosophies of "late Heidegger" and "late Wittgenstein".

The category of intersubjectivity, no less than categories of objectivity and rationality, expresses complex and diverse cognitive intuitions. On the one hand, it assumes a question how the mono-subjectively given world can be shared in its unanimous sense by many individuals. Descartes's metaphysics, weighing on modern thought, makes any answer to this question rely on highly speculative assumptions and assertions. Leibniz thought that monads do not communicate and external orders are derivatives of the pre-established harmony. In Husserl's concept, the problem of intersubjectivity involve the task to overcome the obstacle of "transcendental solipsism", outside phenomenology utterly unknown as a form of the intersubjectivity problem. This issue can be seen still otherwise when we ask about such a way of functioning of objectivised products of culture, that they have a relatively durable ability to retain meanings, at least defying the constraints of mono-subjectivity. Their recognition, using them, would constitute a test of different individuals' social "compatibility". Here in turn we can see the neo-positivist, methodologically narrowed version of the question about the relation between subjective and individual experience with language binding for all rational subjects of cognition.

Although the problem of intersubjectivity is rarely asked directly in the area of sociology,[186] it is constantly present there, *implicite* and synonymically:

All basic ontic (static and dynamic) categories of professional sociology are synonyms of intersubjectivity in an etymological sense: from social relations, social structure, social awareness, social group, social bond etc. to the society

186 Cf. Richard M. Zaner, *Solitude and Society: The Critical Foundations of Social Science*, G. Psathas (eds) *Phenomenology and Sociology*, Wiley-Interscience New York 1973, pp. 25-46.

(community) itself; from social interactions, not excluding basic social processes, like technically understood socialisation etc., to the general notion of socialisation; not to mention the broad idea of "culture", which is the quintessence of all meanings of "intersubjectivity".[187]

Following this reasoning, we must conclude that in sociology the issue of intersubjectivity is as primordial as the problems of objectivity and rationality. Moreover, links between them are visible only when we consider the ontic dimension of these categories. In the area of social sciences, the question about objectivity and rationality cannot be asked with no relation to the question of intersubjectivity.[188] All three questions meet only in their onto-epistemological interpretation.

Here we have to do with the following takes on the issue of intersubjectivity: creation and sharing of a common world not only by co-cognition, but also by co-operation; availability of the Other (*Alter ego*) to investigation, but also creation of the Other through practices and participation in them; conditions of maintaining the society's and culture's coherence as an environment shaping individuality, but also the basis of the possibility to creatively shape that environment thanks to knowledge at different agents' disposal; modes that the shared world is given in as *a priori* common and providing a base for self-awareness, but also producing subjectivity self-separating in the world of actions as a pole of interaction. These are the fundamental forms of philosophical understanding of the intersubjectivity problem, which find continuation in social sciences and where ontological and epistemological moments make up a correlated system, sometimes with prevalent ontological accents, at other times epistemological ones. To capture them in a common social space, I suggest referring to three planes of intersubjectivity: communication, work and fight. On each of these three planes, the dynamics of intersubjectivity is an effect of tension in the

187 Helena Kozakiewicz, *Racjonalność i intersubiektywność. Epistemologiczne wyzwanie dla socjologii i filozofii (Rationality and Intersubjectivity. Epistemological challenges for Sociology and Philosophy)*, in: *Racjonalność współczesności. Między filozofią a socjologią (Rationality of Contemporaneity. Between Philosophy and Sociology)*, ed. Helena Kozakiewicz, Edmund Mokrzycki, Marek J. Siemek, PWN, Warszawa 1992, p. 113.
188 As was proven by Znaniecki, Schütz, Habermas and others.

bipolar system of activities involving subordination and coordination of actions. The primordial character of intersubjectivity depends exactly on the fact that action cannot avoid that bipolarity: it is always efficient when it subordinates and coordinates at the same time, and loses its efficiency when it approaches one of the two poles. Both moments of an agent's relation with its human and non-human environment assume forms of both action and investigation, so they are subordination and coordination of both representations of life environment and activities in it. That is why their links always have an onto-epistemological sense.

Nowadays, the problem of intersubjectivity has already crossed the horizon of epistemological interpretations. When Habermas asks about conditions of joining one agent's actions to other agent's,[189] he transplants traditionally epistemological notions to the ground of notions recognised as a branch of practical philosophy (philosophy of an acting subject). It is an important and meaningful moment, as it steps beyond epistemocentrism in the direction of ontology. However, Habermas is still attached to the transcendental way of interpreting the problem and averse to Heidegger's fundamental ontology, despite being critical to the tradition of early modern philosophy, which exposes the privileges of epistemology. His access to the community of philosophers placed by Taylor on the side of already "overcome" epistemology,[190] is doubtful.[191]

Habermas sees the issue of rationality in reference to intersubjectivity as the fundamental idea of social sciences. The consequence of the privilege endowed to the subject-object relation in philosophy of consciousness is elaborating a model of cognitive-instrumental rationality, and this is assessed by Habermas as inadequate and narrowed. That is why he proposes a model of communicative rationality, which I have already mentioned in the chapter on onto-epistemology of rationality. Habermas's theory of communicative rationality, if not directly, seems to refer to Fichte's model, not Hegel's, which reveals its weakness. The Hegelian model

189 Cf. Habermas, *The Theory of Communicative Action*, pp. 286-287.
190 Cf. Taylor, *Overcoming Epistemology*, pp. 1-19
191 What is significant here is the critique of Foucault's "ontology of ourselves" in: Jürgen Habermas, *The Philosophical Discourse of Modernity. Twelve Lectures*, trans. F. Lawrence, Blackwell Publishers, Oxford 1998, pp. 238-265.

of fight would correspond with the cognitive-instrumental rationality model, which he reconstructs and criticises, and with the concept of strategic action ("monological management"). In contrast, the Fichtean model would find its expression in Habermas's own concept of communicative action. Nevertheless, it is single-minded and problematic that Habermas deems communicative activity "the paradigmatic form of activity in general".[192] Still, he readdresses the problem in a valuable way, describing what he does as "a change of paradigm within action theory: from goal-directed to communicative action",[193] hence a passage from the notion of cognitive-instrumental rationality to the notion of communicative rationality. How does it change the concept of intersubjectivity? ["The focus of investigation thereby shifts from cognitive-instrumental rationality to communicative rationality. And what is paradigmatic for the latter is not the relations of a solitary subject to something in the objective world that can be represented and manipulated, but the intersubjective relations that speaking and acting subjects take up when they come to an understanding with one another about something. [...] In contrast to »representation« or »cognition«, coming to an »understanding« requires the adjective »uncoerced«, because the expression is meant to be used here as a normative concept."[194] It is clearly visible that Habermas avoids the Kantian language, the language of "powers", i.e. describing the issue in subordination categories.

The problem we encounter here is that Habermas's theory of reaching rational consensus is largely constrained to the theory of discursive practice. He views intersubjectivity through doubly narrow lens: as an effect of coordination of discursive activities, and at the same time as an effect of consent on meaning achieved in discourse. The community is constituted by overcoming communicational obstacles, so it does not work both where these practices have a different (non-discursive) character and where the will to communicate gets exhausted while intersubjectivity is retained. We must have in mind that discursive activity aimed at reaching consensus can

---

192 Cf. Kaniowski, *Filozofia społeczna Jürgena Habermasa,* pp. 354-382.
193 Cf. Habermas, *The Theory of Communicative Action,* p. 391.
194 Habermas, *The Theory of Communicative Action,* pp. 391-392.

be undertaken in conditions determined by results of actions whose consensual sense is maintained exactly in order for the discursive sense to be able to appear at all. Hence, discourse does not have and cannot have a character of transcendental reflection on conditions of understanding, which can be applied independently of the entry conditions of discourse. Then, although claims to truth, rightness and sincerity have a presupposed character, that is, their recognition and recognition of a discourse participant's right to them are necessary conditions of success in communicative activity in the form of discourse, creating a situation in which such coordination of claims is really met, does not have a presupposed character. So, claims may be the same, but the assessment whether they are met may be completely different, as it is related to qualifications of intersubjectivity which do not depend on understanding it as a consequence of coordination actions. Communication as an effect of fight or work (where the effect of subordination is possibly more visible) is equally primordial, volatile, but always based on intersubjectivity, just like the communication that emerges in discourse.

Trying to build an onto-epistemological model of intersubjectivity, determined by conditions described above, we can use the analogy to the concepts of a field and a domain in physics. A field in the sense used in physics, created by charges and lines of forces determining behaviour of particles, is unbounded, and each activity in the field entails an effect. A field's main characteristic is the ability to affect everything that is located in it. Any presence in the field causes an effect. In physics, a field in the most general view is an area of the potential activity of forces, which is significant because intersubjectivity, if we include work and fight in its conceptualisation, requires taking forces into account.

The analogy to a physical field in social reality can be sketched like this: an "interactional field" is made up of a socially (not physically!) open space of interactions, which contains both influences by meanings, modifying human thoughts, and practical influences, that is, those modifying other people's behaviours. A field's openness is freedom of actions in the sense of the lack of a natural task.

In turn, a domain in the sense assumed in physics, is a field closed (dominated) by the way of integrating charges which the domain orders; it is always a local area of force, relatively closed, always having determined boundaries. To describe such a field, with multiple centres of ordering, it is enough to distinguish domains understood as areas of closed influences in its area, a determinant of potentials in every object which is in it. A domain is sometimes an area of emancipation, emergence and domination of new qualities and fencing off from the external central forces. Just as life has become a domain in the field of the cosmic law of levelling temperatures, in the field of biological laws a domain of social forces has appeared.

In onto-epistemology, the interactional domain would be a domain of ordered and ordering social forces, an order in the field brought by directions of forces coordinating and subordinating actions of symbolic and practical character. The interactional domain is simply an area of practice, a terrain of activities always restricted by the relation of coordination and subordination of actions, open enough for cognition and knowledge to play a role in it, and simultaneously closed in a way forcing a specific social form upon activities. It is practice, but seen from the perspective of action order intersubjectivity.

Today, there is an important question: is there any centre of a domain determined by modernity, any potential dominant in it? Undoubtedly religion, politics and science have aspired to such a role in the past. Maybe due to the future-oriented culture in modern, or "late modern" societies, there is no such a single centre. Nowadays we would have to talk about a network structure of the intersubjectivity domain, about its polycentric character, which gives it a vivid and flexible form, constantly in a process of redefinition, in a lean towards the future, anyway, with no permanent centre; in the physical analogy surely more similar to a cloud than to a planetary system.

The dynamics of network intersubjectivity, which is captured in the form of a social domain, involves forces of three inseparable (but distinguishable) components: co-operation (i.e. work), hostile confrontation of behaviours (i.e. fight) and communication (i.e. the process of overcoming constraints imposed by time and space on co-operation and fight, constraints thwarting effective and unrestricted proliferation of action effects and reinstating understanding/misunderstanding, empathy/distrust, consent/disagreement – bonds of society). Society is a domain of polycentric and multidirectional structure. Communication, fight and work – all these forms of activity are linked by being action (*praxis*), and not production (*techne*). Each interaction, that is, each social fact treated as a modification of the agent, contains these three aspects. Potential of each of these forms of practice, ordered by the domain of active forces (communication, fight and work) is socially determined by coordination and/or subordination of actions.

The creative, ontic aspect of each of these practice forms, its ability to shape identity can be characterised by the distribution of the coordination and subordination vectors in the interactional domain, coordination and subordination of frequently the same social forces.

Work has a practical sense, not exclusively causative, that is, technological, when it changes the active subjects, as opposed to producing material goods. Moments of coordination and subordination present in it, the necessity to coordinate actions and subordinate the matter formed by work, are conditions of its efficiency, as well as identity-creating moments.

Fight (conflict, rivalry, competition) organises the interactional domain in a way contrary to the one taking place at work. Fight directs the vectors of forces of identity-creating coherence (subordination) to the inside of an individual or a group, as a condition of its persistence, and the vectors of action coordination (strategic activity) to the outside, i.e. in reference to the object of activity, the antagonist, the competitor.

Finally, communication is an interactional domain where the distribution of subordination and coordination also has a creative character in reference to subjectivity (identity). It is exchange and coordination of expressions and utterances, signs and symbols. In this sense their coordinative function is a condition of forging an intersubjective and super-individual communitarian sphere of culture. Communicative action is indispensable in its function of coordination for recognising mutual stances and producing consensus. Being a subject in this perspective is nothing else than ability to create a common sphere of meanings through communication and expression. Nevertheless, communicative activity could not be effective without forces with opposite direction, forces of subordination directed into the interior of identity and norming it as a "performer", an executioner of language acts. They subjugate all expressions and utterances to language, whose norms and principles are respected the more precisely, the less consciousness participates in their execution.

The interactional domain ordered by work, fight or communication, always has a significant epistemic component: each subjective act, each action regulated as practice is characterised by something that Habermas perceives only as a trait of strategic activity, namely prediction. Doing something, at the same time I predict the reaction of the other side: in fight I predict the opponent's move, in communication a partner's answer, in work I foresee the co-worker's action. The epistemic moment is a powerful reducer of interactional domains' inevitable ambiguity in reference to each specific action, based on resources of culture, including intellectual culture. In each action, as long as it belongs to one of interactional domains, an individual is subject to vectors of coordination or subordination.

Intersubjectivity is a practical form of society, a manner of existence for a human community. Unlike a herd, a crowd, a mass and similar collectives it assumes the form of interactional domains ordered by work, fight and communication, each of which forms a whole and marks its boundaries in a way assuming an order of forces that coordinate and subordinate actions, forces subjugated to activity and ordering activity. That is why human beings entangled in intersubjectivity can alternately play active and reactive roles, roles of subjects and objects of practices.

Intersubjectivity is a category primarily related to action, not consciousness. Each action has its boundary, each boundary marks a boundary for another action. Thus action retains the memory of its past, although not necessarily in the form of a conscious experience.

Interactional domains as ordered forms of the intersubjectivity field are areas where interweaving forces of coordination and subordination do not mechanically assign people tasks. Quite the opposite, they allow various degrees of freedom in motivation, as well as their course and effects. However, suppression of any domain in social life changes the whole social structure and dynamics. Dynamics of intersubjectivity triggers forces, models advantages and balances, establishes monopolies and resistances, assumes constructions and destructions in social reality.

Chapter IV Polish Contribution: Ossowski and Znaniecki in View of Social Onto-Epistemology

There is a special feature of the relation between social sciences and philosophical meta-reflection concerning these sciences: it is not clearly determined which issues have a meta-theoretical character and which are strictly scientific. Not only unclear is which areas of social theory can be qualified as objects of above-mentioned types of reflection, but also what kind of relation links them and what motivates to constantly problematise the relations between them. When we adopt an interpretation compliant with the most influential traditions of modern philosophy, we face a certain inconsequence: we assume two separate levels of reflection (epistemological and epistemic), and yet at the same time they are intermingled.[195] From the point of view of different varieties of epistemological fundamentalism, two verdicts are virtually reached in advance: this intermingling is seen as a source of knowledge failures awaiting a researcher in the field of social sciences, and the possibility to take an onto-epistemological view is marginalised. It stems from the one-dimensional problem description. This one dimension only includes critique of knowledge in the Kantian vein and interpretation of its possible results in the area of social studies. On the one hand, it seems that such an interpretation advances the most efficient way of linking science with philosophy: in view of social sciences' insecure status, epistemological (in the sense referring to the epistemic/ epistemological opposition) validation of these sciences would allow to include them smoothly in the modern order of scientific knowledge. This

---

195 Cf. Marek J. Siemek, *Transcendentalizm jako stanowisko epistemologiczne* (*Transcendentalism as an Epistemological Stance*), in: *Dziedzictwo Kanta. Materiały z sesji Kantowskiej* (*Kant's Legacy. Materials from the Kantian Session*), ed. Jan Garewicz, PWN, Warszawa 1976, pp. 17-57. Cf. also Andrzej Lisak, *Marek J. Siemek and His Interpretation of the Idea of Transcendentalism*, "Dialogue and Universalism" 2016, no. 26(2), pp. 205-216.

is, however, where the problem lies, as on the other hand, the categories of the classically construed cognitive relation: "subject (knowledge) – object" cannot be included in this relation without major complications. In social sciences "subject" and "knowledge" must be located on the side of the object, because subjects' studious activities are a significant element of a specific social bond. Epistemocentrism only exacerbates the paradoxes of reflectivity in self-awareness and self-knowledge.

In the field of social sciences, this intermingling can be seen especially distinctly in two situations: the first, where critique determined with a correlation of facts (the epistemic level) and conditions of their possibility (the epistemological level) leans towards knowledge sociology exercised in the Mannheim manner; the second, where sociology declares access to the phenomenological orientation in philosophy, or to other orientations (e.g. in the concept of symbolic interactionism, ethnomethodology), where concepts of subjectivity inherited from philosophy are adopted – concepts based on the assumption that *ego* is experienced in a mono-subjective way, and they are combined with an empirically available way of learning about social relations. This is how simultaneously philosophical and sociological "theoretical hybrids" come into being, when either the notion of subject or the notion of knowledge elaborated on philosophical ground is transferred into scientific research, into the domain of intersubjectively available and historically mutable social phenomena, open to empirical investigation.

On the one hand, such concepts lose their philosophical motivation, since they cease to focus on the main purpose of philosophical critique (from Kant to Husserl), i.e. validation of knowledge, especially scientific knowledge. In such "hybridised", philosophical and empirical concepts knowledge is considered not in its normative or truth-establishing aspect, but as a social fact. As such, it does not have any validating power, apart from "quasi-validation" subjugated to ideology. Its critique, whether Marx and Engels-style, or in the vein of Habermas, does not lead to the issue of validation construed epistemologically. Knowledge is treated here as a kind of social epiphenomenon, whose critique has a rather emancipative than epistemological sense. Thus this form of critique is hard to accept for epistemologists. This is testified to by incessant counter-critiques of both sociology of knowledge and sociological concepts akin to them (P. Winch), performed from epistemocentric positions.[196] They focus on proving relativist and catch-22 consequences, unacceptable for epistemocentric stances. Meanwhile, more radical opponents of such understanding of the issue, aware of the paradox inherent in epistemological critique which assumes one of its results at the point of entry (e.g. Giddens) tend to transgress the cognitive perspective of social sciences, towards the hermeneutical principle formulated by Heidegger: that the problem is not how to leave the vicious circle of interpretations based on interpretations, but how to enter this circle.[197]

On the other hand, the intermingling described above appears in a different form when we have to do with movement opposite to the above. It depends on introducing the concept of subject coined from philosophy into the sociological discourse. Such constructions as the division between "I" and "me" (like in G.H. Mead's work) or engaging the phenomenological notion of subject in sociological analysis (as in A. Schütz's research) lead to difficulties of another kind: subjects' ability to learn about themselves is empirically uncapturable and the opposition of knowledge and activity keeps re-emerging. These problems make fulfilment of so oriented social study's scientific aspirations more difficult. Philosophical critics of such portrayals propose abandoning epistemology on the base of widely construed social study, in favour of a certain practical involvement of philosophy (as did R. Rorty) or (like K. Popper) retaining the significance of epistemology for social sciences by redefining problems of social practice in terms of social technology.[198]

However, this kind of meta-reflection's entanglement into scientific issues and of scientific issues into philosophical meta-reflection can assume the form of critique unrelated to the tradition of modern philosophy of

---

196 This is the case of Popper's critique of knowledge sociology, as well as critics of Winch's concept.
197 Cf. Martin Heidegger, *Being and Time*, trans. Joan Stambaugh, State University of New York Press, Albany 1996.
198 Cf. Richard Rorty, *Philosophy and the Mirror of Nature*, Princeton University Press, Princeton, New Jersey 1979, pp. 129-311; Karl R. Popper, *The Logic of the Social Sciences*; idem, *The Open Society and its Enemies*: Volume 1: *The Spell of Plato*, Princeton University Press, Princeton, New Jersey 1971, pp. 18-34, 157-168.

subject. It is a form of critique understood as analysis of social sciences' research strategies according to standards of the ideal of scientific knowledge determined by the modern form of science. It is that ideal, woven into the standards of critical discourse, that establishes the epistemocentric character of that critique. Another question is about the boundaries of valid knowledge. It is asked not because of the confinement of the subject's condition, constituting their ability to acquire knowledge. It is asked from the point of view of a specific research area's disciplinary autonomy. In this case, epistemocentrism stems not from the philosophical assumptions concerning the " subject – cognition – object of cognition" relation. It assumes another form: a critical analysis of research strategies adopted by science in its specific character and disciplinary identity.

1. Ossowski's road to onto-epistemology

A good example of such analysis is the treatise *O osobliwościach nauk społecznych (Special Characteristics of the Social Sciences)*, by Polish philosopher and sociologist Stanisław Ossowski.[199] There he proposes a meta-theoretical discourse in relation to "widely understood" sociology. The meaning of the discourse depends on showing its specific character, its distinctiveness from other sciences. Thus, without restrictive zeal, he marks the disciplinary boundaries of sociology, and, to a degree, he suspends the

---

199 Cf. Stanisław Ossowski, *O osobliwościach nauk społecznych* [*Special Characteristics of the Social Sciences*] PWN, Warszawa 1967. See also: Maria Bielińska-Hirszowicz, *Reviewed Work:* O osobliwościach nauk społecznych [Special Characteristics of the Social Sciences] *by Stanisław Ossowski,* "The Polish Sociological Bulletin" 1963, no. 8, pp. 115-117; Mariola Kuszyk-Bytniewska, *Osobliwości nauk społecznych a związki między filozofią i socjologią. Florian Znaniecki a Stanisław Ossowski (Special Characteristics of the Social Sciences and Relationships between Philosophy and Sociology. Florian Znaniecki and Stanislaw Ossowski),* in: *Koncepcje socjologiczne Stanisława Ossowskiego a teoretyczne i praktyczne zagadnienia współczesności (Stanisław Ossowski's Sociological Ideas versus Theoretical and Practical Issues of the Present Day),* red. Mirosław Chałubiński, Janusz Goćkowski, Iwona Kaczmarek-Murzyniec, Anna Woźniak, Biblioteka „Colloquia Communia" (47), Wydawnictwo Adam Marszałek, Toruń 2004, pp. 173-187; Mirosław Chałubiński, *Stanisław Ossowski,* Wiedza Powszechna, Warszawa 2007, pp. 24-64.

question of epistemological foundations. The key to this strategy is the eponymous "special characteristics of the social sciences". The use of the term is no coincidence. It is a terminological loan from analyses that Tadeusz Kotarbiński made in a short chapter of his *Elementy teorii poznania, logiki formalnej i metodologii nauk (Elements of Epistemology, Formal Logic and Science Methodology)* about historical sciences.[200] Kotarbiński, inadvertently yet philosophically non-neutrally, in the epistemocentric spirit, expressed the conviction of the "non-special" sciences' general form, that of proper, normal and ordinary sciences. Kotarbiński does not reject, then, and neither does Ossowski, the scientific aspirations of "critical, practical, normative disciplines".[201] He discusses their peculiar condition and possibly epistemological helplessness. Recalling Aristotle's loose definition of science,[202] Kotarbiński opens the gate for critique which finds its proper area in the similarities and differences between special sciences (disciplines) and non-special ones (it is tempting to say "normal"). The formula of connecting purely cognitive and practical skills, as Kotarbiński calls them, is no less special.[203] Ossowski follows these imperatives, making up a moderate form of epistemocentrism.

Science in this perspective, as a research discipline, is normed by an array of not only methodological verdicts, which let it separate the studious effort and the value of its results from their direct practical contexts, i.e. social contexts. Sciences which require weakening this condition are perceived as special, peculiar. Here we can see that Kotarbiński and Ossowski share a common approach to social sciences, rooted in beliefs emblematic

---

200 Tadeusz Kotarbiński, *Dzieła wszystkie*, t. I: *Elementy teorii poznania, logiki formalnej i metodologii (Collected Works, vol. I: Elements of Epistemology, Formal Logic and Methodology)*, Ossolineum Wydawnictwo PAN, 1990, p. 389.
201 Kotarbiński, *Elementy teorii poznania, logiki formalnej i metodologii*, p. 412.
202 Kotarbiński says: „Maybe it would be best to talk about critical, practical, normative »disciplines« (from the Latin *disciplina*, derivated from *disco* - »I learn«), by discipline meaning »what can be taught and learnt«", p. 412.
203 Cf. Kotarbiński, *Elementy teorii poznania, logiki formalnej i metodologii*, pp. 413-414.

of their intellectual environment, which is the Lwów-Warsaw School.[204] The norm of social sciences, and at the same time their disciplinary characteristic, according to such a concept, is some kind of inevitable difficulty, a kind of "theoretical clinamen" that should be methodologically and meta-theoretically exposed. Furthermore, the results of insights executed this way should be analytically purified in order to grant the knowledge created within these sciences access to the scientific circuit, with explicitly expressed restrictions and validity clauses. Social sciences, facing the threat of collapse under the burden of basically non-scientific motives or the threat of exclusion from the realm of sciences, constantly must verify their cognitive status, but they must also protect the boundaries of their territory, their discipline. This is, it seems, the idea of Ossowski's book.[205]

What is the source of this incessant meta-discourse in social sciences, at times assuming the form of controversy, and at times that of competent exchange of arguments? How does it shape the theoretical awareness of these sciences? How does the content of these very sciences participate in it? What, in view of social realities, motivates the question about the status of sociology as a science, about its scientificity and autonomy?

Ossowski deals with these issues in an analytical way. He confronts charges pressed against social sciences with peculiarities which may be thought, rightly or not, to motivate cognitive strategies whose inevitable results, risky for the value of knowledge, are the said peculiarities. This way he discusses and diagnoses the epistemological condition of sociology and its weaker position among sciences. Although the text appeared over half a century ago, it remains thought-provoking.

The epistemocentric orientation of Ossowski's analyses is visible at the first glance, and it is more conspicuous in the lack of certain definitions of its departure point, than in positive statements. Namely, Ossowski does not write about the sources and extra-theoretical entanglements of social sciences, save the enigmatic hint at their "practical tasks". However, he

---

204 Cf. The Lvov-Warsaw School and Contemporary Philosophy, ed. Katarzyna Kijania-Placek, Jan Woleński, Springer Science & Business Media, Dordrecht 1998.

205 Cf. Kuszyk-Bytniewska, *Osobliwości nauk społecznych a związki między filozofią i socjologią. Florian Znaniecki a Stanisław Ossowski*, pp. 173-187.

traces the latter to the antiquity with no respect to differences in their historic ways of understanding and real functioning. Hence modernity, as the era when sociology and its subject came into being, for him is not the turning point in the history of social sciences, let alone the departure point of the analyses he presented. This does not mean that Ossowski generally discounts the historicity of social phenomena and the historicity of knowledge concerning them. Nevertheless, while distinguishing the link between modernity as a certain socio-historical reality, with scientific ideas developed within it, he refers to economics, as opposed to sociology. This does not mean either, that Ossowski does not notice the specific relation between social sciences' subject of study and these sciences' theoretical situation, i.e. their involvement in the subject of study. His point of view is doubly confined, though. First of all, he consequently sees these peculiarities as obstacles for gaining full knowledge and as limitations of the method's efficiency, either due to the researcher's cognitive situation, or due to the specific subject matter, or due to the specific relation between them. Therefore, it is justified to suspect that according to Ossowski, there are "non-special" sciences, that is ones that do not suffer from such impediments. More essentially, he seems to state that these peculiarities do not play positive roles in study, i.e. neither do they contribute to the method's efficiency, nor do they belong to the conditions of cognition. Secondly, these links do not constitute peculiarities of the very cognitive acts. They only specify (by limiting) the value of their results. Thus Ossowski does not propose any epistemology of immature sciences, but he collectively treats the peculiarities of social sciences as sources of their immaturity, some of whom only have a historic significance, while others lie immanently in their theoretical situation.

The main historic factor of social sciences' immaturity is their insufficiently formed disciplinary autonomy. Hence, Ossowski begins from considering the condition of sociology as science, discussed as the phenomenon of "sociology's scientific underdevelopment" caused by its "retardation". The retardation of sociology is, on the one hand, an effect of sociology's dependence on non-scientific factors and intellectual needs: (based on common sense and ideology, like fostering social preferences or forging social tendencies). On the other hand, it stems from limitations of its autonomy rooted in the relation with other disciplines. The latter is caused by inevitably blurred borders between different domains of social sciences.[206]

The second kind of charges against sociology, consistent with the critique of its retardation, is a historical refurbishment of the first one: it concerns sociology's "double birth certificate". Namely, sociology appeared in early 19th century as a separate discipline, largely just postulated and speculative, and it re-emerged only at the turn of the 19th century as an empirical science, slowly fencing off from philosophy (more precisely, from metaphysics), devoted to seeking empirical laws. As a matter of fact, it is about two issues: the issue of differences in treating their own pedigrees by the community of scholars, which leads to different concepts of sociology,[207] as well as the issue of the discipline's "improper" history, that is, the lack of continuity in its history and the disrupted accumulation of achievements in the process of knowledge production.[208]

This state of affairs is shaped, on the one hand, by the social sciences' long prehistory, which can be almost arbitrarily reached for as anticipation of its supposedly "proper" form. On the other hand, it stems from the indeterminate character and diversity of concepts concerning the purposes of research, which also affect diverse attitudes to tradition. For example, we have Durkheim's concept of sociology as an autonomous research discipline, autonomous with respect to the subject and specific in its methods. Then, we have a concept initiated in the 20th century: sociology as exact, empirical science about society, practised according to methodological models elaborated in empirical sciences. The former mostly seeks disciplinary autonomy, while the latter strives to contribute to the growth of knowledge capable of effective application. Both concepts also spawn socially different types of sociologists and different research stances: a reinventor of social orders and an uninvolved investigator. Therefore, they are difficult to reconcile.[209] So sociology is characterised by double methodological model, a kind of methodological ambivalence: it can be

---

206 Cf. Ossowski, O osobliwościach nauk społecznych, pp. 131-137.
207 Cf. Ossowski, O osobliwościach nauk społecznych, pp. 137-141.
208 Cf. Ossowski, O osobliwościach nauk społecznych, pp. 110-114.
209 Cf. Ossowski, O osobliwościach nauk społecznych, pp. 110-130.

practised as a humanist science or adhere to the methodological standards of natural and empirical sciences.

Another type of specificity (peculiarity) is rooted in the very social phenomena as objects of investigation. Ossowski sees their peculiarity in such characteristics of the subjects studied by sociology that do not have a counterpart in the area of natural sciences. Above all, these are: (1) the long observed influence of research results on reality that those results mean to describe, (2) direct influence of the very research activities on the investigated reality, (3) the conflict between the postulate of systematic research and the postulate of seeking general conclusions, unbounded by historical circumstances, (4) the conflict between adherence to standardised methods on the one hand, and subtlety of investigated problems, as well as the chosen indicators' power of description, (5) the involvement of internal experience in research problems."[210]

All these peculiarities are indeed either forms of onto-epistemological entanglement of social phenomena, or their consequences. Each case is about some form of shaping social phenomena, whose specific character manifests in their dependence on the knowledge of different subjects and influence that knowledge exerts on those subjects by gathering and using to carry out complex technological and practical activities. It is, then, about a situation where being the knowledge-seeking agent becomes a necessary factor of the agent's recognisability as a social actor, and possibly, an agent responsible for practical or technological action. In order to participate in a specific activity, either one must have some kind of knowledge, including knowledge shared with others, or having knowledge of a specified kind is a determinant of the agent's recognisability as a participant in social life. In one way or another, knowledge determined by a subjective functor becomes an indispensable element of analyses concerning social phenomena.

Thus, the feedback that investigation results cause in social reality (that these results concern) is an example of a "self-fulfilling prophecy" or a "self-cancelling prophecy". The same kind of factors that are present in these "prophecies" prevent a sociologist from repeating the investigation.

---

210 Ossowski, O osobliwościach nauk społecznych, p. 147.

First, a repeated investigation takes place in socially changed conditions. Second, the more thorough the research, the more the departure point of successive investigations changes under the influence of earlier results. Hence, interpretations constitute an inevitable part of an interpreted reality, and the very act of measurement (investigation) affects a measured (investigated) object.[211] For example, questions about declared religious values can make the respondent aware that values indeed exist as an object of a possible reference.

Adopting the stance of an interpreter enforces a variable "participation of research experience in investigated problems". The more we demand generality of research results, experience becomes a non-methodical participant of study, which burdens the research with uncertainty. As Ossowski says: "We need either to abandon methods or wide generalisations".[212]

In a sociologist's research practice, says Ossowski, the part of internal experience is important. That performs a heuristic function, it helps to interpret people's utterances and actions, explains mechanisms of an interactional bond referring to motivation, as well as supports (*explicite* or *implicite*) justifying general statements "when observation material is not sufficient to perform verification meeting scientific requirements".[213] The difference between a sociologist-humanist and a sociologist-radical empiricist is that the former allows all functions of internal experience,[214] while the latter is restricted to the first one, that is, the heuristic function of internal experience. Humanistic sociology draws from Aristotelian ethics, where study of (social) reality is achieved by action, as opposed to observation. Conversely, radically empirical sociology, seeking methodological models in natural sciences, affirms that to gain insight into reality a researcher must stick strictly to observation and disinvolvement. Empiricism turns the notion of insight into observation and a researcher is meant to remain an observer of phenomena, impossible to knock off balance like a

---

211 A similar effect discovered in quantum mechanics gave rise to an epistemological debate in physics, and Heisenberg's uncertainty principle seemed an impassable research barrier.
212 Ossowski, O osobliwościach nauk społecznych, p. 155.
213 Ossowski, O osobliwościach nauk społecznych, p. 167.
214 Ossowski, O osobliwościach nauk społecznych, pp. 164-171.

rock. When we choose the first option, peculiarities of social sciences must be employed in research, with the inevitable risk for their results. In the second option, in turn, they must be analytically purified, accepting the inherent risk that the results may be banal. Ossowski, in my opinion, leaned towards the first option.

However, Ossowski does not discuss these specific properties of sociological research as involvement in ontic moments of the cognitive situation. So he abandons the perspective in which we can notice properties of sociological knowledge allowing it to influence reality that this knowledge concerns, and properties of that reality allowing it to be affected with that knowledge. Therefore he does not investigate the practical meaning of studious activities concerning social life. Neither does he try to specify the ontic ground of the conflict between generality and concreteness of results. He does not analyse the inevitable part of internal experience from the perspective of ontic location of the subject as a simultaneous knowledge seeker and a participant of social activities.

Basically, two reasons contribute to Ossowski's abandonment of the research direction that we could qualify as onto-epistemological. The first one is blindness to the difference between practice and technology, characteristic for epistemocentrism. As a result, Ossowski accepts the order of ideas which validates this blindness, the order where practice is application, embodiment of an idea, a manner of action or thinking. The second reason is rejection or simply overlooking of the theoretical opportunity for social sciences provided by the perspective of hermeneutics. It is a result of qualifying the analysed entanglements of social sciences as no more than impediments to knowledge, while at the same time thanks to them knowledge can be acquired. Hence Ossowski sees the interpretability of social phenomena as a negative effect of these limitations, imposing the form of disciplinary singularity on social research. That has a decisive effect on the inextricably tentative value of sociology's research results.

So, is it worthwhile to apply models of natural sciences to social phenomena? If we assume that autonomy of the discipline is a value Ossowski pursues, then the price of "peculiarity" paid by sociology for that value, the price of "theoretical clinamen" is, in his view, acceptable. This means abandoning the idea of natural science as a model for social sciences, but also acceptance of theoretical weaknesses and permanent immaturity of the latter. Although over half a century has elapsed since Ossowski's book was released, peculiarities of sociology (especially those concerning properties of its objects) still play an ambivalent role in it; they both inspire investigation (*vide* A. Giddens's double hermeneutics[215]) and sow doubt concerning these sciences' status.

Consequently, contrary to Ossowski's view, it is not the issue of the discipline's immaturity. It is rather about the way social sciences establish their disciplinary autonomy and their place among other disciplines. From the point of view of onto-epistemology it is about the evident, inextricable presence of the philosophical meta-discourse in social sciences, the discourse indispensable for gaining insight into the peculiarities of investigated objects. These peculiarities appear as such only when we consider early modern paradigms of scientificity as dominant and necessary to settle where and how the boundaries between sciences run. Only from that level can we see the inextricable characteristics (as peculiarities) of sociology's subject and, in consequence, peculiarity of research approaches which can yield any valuable results. Ossowski was perfectly aware of it, though the intellectual tradition he was rooted in prevented him from assuming onto-epistemological definitions of studied problems. Epistemocentrism lay in his stance of a researcher-sociologist and a philosopher-sociology analyst as an irremovable obstacle for a possible onto-epistemological reorientation of his research.

A different kind of research approach can be found in the work of another scholar of double, sociological and philosophical, provenance: Florian Znaniecki, who followed a path consistent with the spirit of social onto-epistemology.

2. Znaniecki's reflexive onto-epistemology

Florian Znaniecki is known primarily as the creator of original and influential sociological theories (culturalism), notions (humanistic coefficient) and research tools (the autobiographical method, co-invented with Thomas). He was also one of the first (alongside Mannheim and Scheler)

---

215 Cf. Anthony Giddens, *The Constitution of Society. Outline of the Structuration*, University of California Press, Berkeley, Los Angeles 1984.

initiators of knowledge sociology. Like Ossowski, he was a philosopher, too, which profoundly influenced his sociological concepts. He understood that philosophy and social science need to be strongly linked. Unsolved or erroneously solved philosophical problems lead either to wrong theoretical choices or to paradoxes. Even worse is a scholar's unawareness of his/her theory's and empirical research's entanglement in strong philosophical presuppositions. However, while Ossowski came to consider philosophical problems only as a mature scholar, in the case of Znaniecki an attempt to delimit the periods of philosophical and separate sociological activity in his work would be artificial.[216] Those who try to separate Znaniecki's philosophy from his sociology most often use a chronological criterion to classify his work (earlier work was in the field of philosophy, later in the field of sociology) or the criterion of language (most of Znaniecki's philosophical work was written in Polish and most of his sociological work in English).[217] It is, though, an artificial division, since Znaniecki treated his philosophical considerations as complementary to scientific ones and equally important. What is more, the philosophical stance he reached had its consequences for formulating sociological problems. Although he remained under the influence of post-Kantian philosophical thought, including both transcendental programmes of validating humanist sciences and positivist programmes of reducing knowledge to science, he was critical to philosophical traditions that supported sociology known to him. At the same time he was convinced that grafting neo-Kantian and neo-positivist philosophy on the sociological ground would not bring favourable results. Among philosophical traditions that he accepted and to which he succumbed, he mentioned pragmatism and, quite unexpectedly for the

216 Cf. Janina Markiewicz-Lagneau, *Florian Znaniecki: Polish Sociologist or American Philosopher?* "International Sociology" 1988, vol. 3, no. 4, pp. 385-402.
217 Note that his *Cultural Reality* from 1919, in my opinion his main philosophical work, was written in English and released in Chicago, while *Wstęp do socjologii* (*Introduction to Sociology*, 1922), one of more important sociological works, was written in Polish and released in Warsaw. This, however, does not change the fact that Znaniecki's Polish-language works are barely known outside the country and rarely referred to.

reader of his sociological work, "Polish historical idealism" or "action philosophy".[218]

Thus, Znaniecki's philosophical thought formed in opposition to two basic alternatives: between naturalism and idealism in philosophy, and between positivism and metaphysics in science. However, as a philosopher, he approved of and adopted an anti-naturalistic, anti-psychologist and anti-fundamentalist methodological stance in the area of epistemology.[219] Most significantly, in expression of the most original aspect of his theoretical achievements, he also created pluralistic ontology of social being. Originality of his humanist coefficient concept, the concept of social action, theory of values or knowledge sociology lose a lot when they are considered out of the context provided by the whole theoretical dimension of his work. Znaniecki held that the main obstacle to doing social sciences (he used the term of *cultural sciences*[220]) is the philosophical tradition of cognition and knowledge embodied by epistemological fundamentalism, as well as epistemocentrically oriented philosophy. He stated that this tradition may be adhered to only within the confines of natural study, and even that for the price of the growing gap between scientific knowledge and principles of philosophy. Social sciences (especially philosophy) compel us to redefine the assumptions underlying the early modern philosophy of subjectivity and knowledge, though. That philosophy did not foresee scientific investigation of social reality. While, as we have realised, sociology's theoretical awareness is entangled in issues involving problematic philosophical verdicts, sociology can be practised only on the prepared ground of philosophy. Thus, Znaniecki adopts an anti-naturalist view (in a methodological sense) that all research of reality must take into account the way acting subjects refer to one another, just as to subjects defined by being conscious. In other words: social theory is compelled to explain social orders created by conscious subjects. It is then not only about people as subjects in action, but also active in experiencing the world; it is

---

218 Cf. Znaniecki, *Cultural Reality*, pp. XIII-XIV.

219 Cf. Norbert Wiley, *Znaniecki's Key Insight: The Merger of Pragmatism and Neo-Kantianism*, "Polish Sociological Review" 2007, vol. 158(2), pp. 133-143.

220 Cf. Florian Znaniecki, *Cultural Sciences. Their Origin and Development*, University of Illinois Press, Urbana 1952.

about subjects who have the possibility to reflectively (consciously) refer to each other and to other "actors" of social life. This, though, requires basic and simultaneously philosophical verdicts. They all boil down to understanding how actors defined by their reflectivity, and consequently excluded from courses of events in the real world can enter (by action and co-operation) the reality of what constitutes the context of action, enter the "concrete reality". This way of thinking is convergent with the onto-epistemological take on the specific character of social sciences, in which ontic definitions of social agency subjects require their ability to consider relations with other subjects.

Znaniecki does not succumb to the anti-metaphysical attitude of contemporaneous thinkers (philosophers and sociologists). He departs from the epistemological perspective of defining primary issues in cultural sciences in favour of ontological thought. He does it to rethink these definitions.[221] In this thought, he sees a basically constructive idea in the face of the fatal alternative between positivism and transcendentalism. He proposes a stance meant to avoid it, calling it culturalism. He uses the notion of "culture" as an emblem of sorts for his own philosophy, as opposed to, say, the notion of "society". I reckon this to be an expression of Znaniecki's philosophical preferences. He attributes special meaning to interactional orders of human actions, as well as orders of their objectivised results in the form of axionormative orders (in Znaniecki's terms). Doing so, he systematically stresses that those orders are not identical, although they complement each other all the time. The main condition of objective, scientific study of social reality is not as much a property of scientific methodology as a property of the object itself, its socially objectivised being. Thanks to this Znaniecki tries to cope with such a concept of cultural and social reality that can include creativity as a basic dimension of all action and thinking. It is then not only about being a "correlate of consciousness", but also about how that being acquires the character of a creative result of human activity, as well as how that result can lead to creative initiative in activity. Therefore Znaniecki's culturalism is an anti-naturalist,

---

221 The ontological revival took place much later but Znaniecki's work ushers in a similar thinking pattern.

anti-idealist and anti-psychologist position when we consider its attitude to philosophical tradition. It is also a position of pluralistic ontology, as he takes up the task of explaining diverse cultural orders in which we participate by action, experiencing and consciousness.

The sense of his own philosophy (culturalism) was seen by Znaniecki in a way characteristic to 19th-century philosophy: humanistic and social sciences require a philosophical validation. However, he rejected both naturalism and idealism as views concerning ontological foundations of cultural reality. He also rejected epistemological fundamentalism and positivism as epistemological premises for the culturalist stance. He wrote: "There are no absolutely new beginnings, no fundamental original truths which a philosopher can find at the outset of his reflection ...".[222] Znaniecki's stance on these issues is contained above all in the theory of "concrete reality", expressing theses on how the subject of cultural sciences exists. On the other hand, it is also visible in the concept of "humanistic coefficient", an ontological and epistemological thesis concerning the way of existence and the proper way of studying culture, as well as in the "action theory", which embodies the culturalist concept of subjectivity.

Concrete reality is reality characterised by reference to experience understood as an ontological category, that is in its entanglement with action. Znaniecki sought a theory of cultural subject construed as an effect of human creative activity, and he understood culture as the domain where this activity is objectivised. Concrete reality is the soil experienced in reflection and in action, the soil giving birth to culture as a correlative-objective entity. This perspective makes oppositions like "being – thought", "existence – essence", "experience – intellect", "idea – reality", "activity – study" merely relative. Concrete reality is both "natural environment" for human activity and experience and the environment of intellectual activity leading to highly abstract theoretical creations produced by reflection. It is a milieu of practical activity and a support for bringing thoughts into reality. Znaniecki gives up on such reconstructions of social world which privilege the transcendental-subjective (epistemocentric) perspective of universal (in the cognitive sense) reference, he gives up on exclusive

---

222 Znaniecki, *Cultural Reality*, p. 23.

defining of the object of reflection (representation, symbolic conceptualisation etc.) in favour of portrayals involving entanglement of perspective in
a certain model of activity. Theoretical thinking, which uses the notion of
"insight" (a notion that empiricism has turned into observation) positions
the researcher as a neutral observer of phenomena. Thus endowing it with
mobility, which the theory of interactional orders requires, may engender
a (false) impression of entailing relativism. As a matter of fact, Znaniecki's
stance is rather existential pluralism understood as an ontological position
assuming multiplicity of manners and degrees of existence.[223] Sociology,
as seen by Znaniecki, has its precedents only in the deep history of social
thought reaching the tradition of Aristotle's "ethics" and "politics" construed exactly as theories of action (*praxis*). Study of (social) reality is
carried out by acting and experiencing, as opposed to observation, and it
participates in this reality (onto-epistemology). A subject is primarily an
agent (a subject of action). Therefore concrete reality is a human environment for both thought and action. In this sense it is a notion analogous to
Husserl's category of *Lebenswelt* (everyday lifeworld). However, the concept of "concrete reality" distinguishes Znaniecki's pluralism and "ontological penchant" from concepts of lifeworld philosophy. Concrete reality
cannot be subjected to any Idea (maybe it is here that Znaniecki revives the
Kantian critique of metaphysics), and in this sense it contains irreducible
diversity. That diversity is not as much diversity of intentional references
of consciousness, which ultimately come together in the agent, as diversity
of manners of existence, degrees of reality, measures of ordering, diversity of heteronomical and heterogeneous definitions of realities given to
subjects by experience, reflection and action.

Cultural objects as objects of investigation and action were described
by Znaniecki as "incomplete", i.e. not entirely determined in their existential status, in their way of existence. An object is incomplete because it

223 Cf. Mariola Kuszyk, *Floriana Znanieckiego koncepcja rzeczywistości
    konkretnej. Przyczynek do nie-Husserlowskiej teorii doświadczenia (Florian
    Znaniecki's Concept of Concrete Reality. A Contribution to non-Husserlian
    Theory of Experience)*, in: *Studia z polskiej myśli filozoficznej 1900-1939
    (Studies on Polish Philosophical Thought 1900-1939)*, ed. Leszek Gawor,
    Wydawnictwo UMCS, Lublin 1997, pp. 39-46.

is not permanently equipped with any existential qualification. Hence it is susceptible to more precise definition by acts of human activity. So, each object can belong to many systems of objects and in its existence it is not determined immanently, but it is redefined every time, on one side by the system of objects which it belongs to, and on the other by acting on it and experiencing it. Thus objects can be redefined in their manners of existence by the objectivising powers of action and thinking. Being an object in cultural reality means being in becoming and in duration dependent on cultural orders (orders of meanings and values) inherited in time, whose existence is enforced by coordination of investigation and action. A cultural object is then defined by its double disposition: being an object of activity and being an element of a cultural order. This double disposition of a cultural object is made possible by its duration, which manifests in concrete reality through meanings and values. The essence of Znaniecki's idea boils down to the statement that duration and extent are revealed and experienced through meanings and values that make up an *axionormative,* cultural order. Hence they are basic, ontological categories of concrete reality allowing to experience that reality in a certain cultural order. They allow to experience meanings and values and to bring them into reality.

The specific character of cultural sciences, according to Znaniecki, lies in the fact that objects of investigation, as results of objectivising activity of humans, are already defined by being given to certain subjects (either as correlates of their consciousness or as products of their practical activity) and, consequently, they belong to specific systems of objects:

> This characteristic of cultural phenomena, objects of humanist research, the fundamental property that, as objects of theoretical reflection, they are already objects given to someone in experience, or someone's conscious actions, can be called a *humanistic coefficient* of these phenomena.[224]

In other words, objects of cultural sciences are equipped with a humanistic coefficient, which means that they are always presented to investigation as "co-data": another consciousness, different from that of the investigator, can experience them or is currently experiencing them in a

---

224 Florian Znaniecki, *Wstęp do socjologii (Introduction to Sociology)*, PWN, Warszawa 1988, p. 25.

sense determined by the *axionormative* order of culture. This way the humanistic coefficient is not only something attributed to a cultural phenomenon. It is also a fundamental property of operators of social actions on these objects, a premise of creative activity, an aspect of what is given and created. These operators, whatever we think of them, are elements of an *axionormative* order. To put it another way: the phenomenological status of "co-data" characterising cultural phenomena is only an aspect of social order which, as an intersubjective one, requires such forms of objectivity that can be provided only by (co-)operating agents.

Therefore, the concept of humanistic coefficient is above all Znaniecki's corollary from considerations of the way cultural reality exists. That entails that it is also, consequently, a methodological directive formulating a rule in investigating culture.[225] That is because according to Znaniecki all reality is endowed with a humanistic coefficient, thus all real objects must be equally reproduced from actuality in cognition, all possible objects are correlates of a subject. Hence, at most this methodological directive can be derived from the concept of humanistic coefficient: research of culture must be conducted with the awareness that the structure of cultural objects

---

225 In the literature of this subject two interpretations of the humanistic coefficient can be found: an epistemological (methodological) one and the ontological one. The former boils down to a directive compelling a researcher of culture to describe all cultural facts and phenomena with a humanistic coefficient, that is, as given to the consciousness of participants in culture. The latter, in turn, can be expressed in a statement that all facts and phenomena of culture exist with a humanistic coefficient, i.e. exist as such, provided that certain consciousnesses or subjectivities are given. The meaning of the epistemological version would be embodied in an answer to the question: what is a humanist allowed to do and what is a naturalist? The meaning of the ontological version, then, would involve the question: what does a humanist investigate and what does a naturalist? However, as Szacki wrote: "In the essence an investigator of culture does not face the choice between investigating culture with a humanistic coefficient and investigating culture without it. According to Znaniecki, culture is either investigated with a humanistic coefficient, or it is not investigated at all, since it eludes any other kind of investigation." (Jerzy Szacki, *Znaniecki*, Wiedza Powszechna, Warszawa 1986, pp. 92-93; see also: Jerzy Szacki, *Historia myśli socjologicznej. Wydanie nowe*, (*History of Sociological Thought*), PWN, Warszawa 2002, pp. 761-763).

contains a humanistic coefficient. In other words, before they become objects of some research, they are already correlates of a subject's activity. Existence of a cultural object depends, among others, on "being given" to a subject. Objects of concrete reality are situated between the boundary of absolute subjectivity and the boundary of absolute objectivity. The latter, approaching the boundary of absolute objectivity, that is, in Znaniecki's terms, belonging to possibly many sufficiently broad object systems, can be investigated without the humanistic coefficient.[226] In this case and only this the humanistic coefficient can be disregarded, i.e. it is unnecessary to take into account the circumstance that real objects are extracted from actuality with no regard to "whose" actuality it is. Thus the humanistic coefficient can be placed in the "space of becoming" on a plane of two co-ordinates: one shown on the axis between subjectivisation and objectivisation, and another between thought and experience. Where an object exists in such a way that its content is doubly dependent, on subjectivisation and experience, the humanistic coefficient cannot be overlooked, whereas when its content approaches full objectivity and purely reflective status, it can be omitted. This makes methodological oppositions: nomothetic vs idiographic sciences, understanding vs explaining, as well as the opposition between values and facts, are rather a question of degree than disjunction.

---

226 This concept reveals significant similarities to the hermeneutical understanding of objectivity as a property of scientific research. Gadamer says: "In this regard scientific experience possesses a unique status. The experience that can be validated as certain by the scientific method has the distinction of being in principle absolutely independent of any situation of action and of every integration into the context of action. This 'objectivity' conversely implies that it is able to serve every such possible context. It is precisely this 'objectivity' which was so quintessentially realized in modern science and which transformed broad expanses of the face of the earth into an artificial human environment. Now the experience which has been reworked by the sciences has, indeed, the merit of being verifiable and acquirable by everyone. But then, in addition, it raises the claim that on the basis of its methodological procedure it is the only certain experience, hence the only mode of knowing in which each and every experience is rendered truly legitimate." Gadamer, *Theory, Technology, Praxis*, in: Gadamer, *The Enigma of Health*, p. 2.

Consequently, reality described by social sciences is not devoid of objectivity, methods of these sciences do not have to lead to relativism. "Objective" means reproduced multiple times in the course of experience and action, belonging to a certain system of objects. "Objective" does not mean "independent of a subject", but breaking free from it through stabilising its (continuously extending) meaning, hence existing as a value. The condition of objectivity in cognition is objectivisation of an object in a system of objects.

Concrete reality is construed by Znaniecki as a process. Objectivity here means belonging to possibly many systems of objects, orders objectivising certain empirical content and a possibility of being given to (experiencing by) possibly many subjects. That is why objects meeting the conditions of objectivity assumed by natural sciences can be investigated without a humanistic coefficient. In their case, one can disregard the circumstance that real objects are extracted from actuality by cognition. In turn, those objects which apart from empirical content also contain cultural meanings and values (proper objects of cultural sciences), must be investigated with a humanistic coefficient, since processes of their objectivisation assume that they must be objects of experience and reflection, as well as action. "A value is different from a thing in having both *content*, which distinguishes it as an empirical object from other objects, and *meaning*, which recalls other subjects that it was actively associated with in the past; a thing does not have a meaning, only content, and represents itself."[227]

The theory of action is complementary to the concept of cultural object, since it poses the question how a human being, as a finite being, refers to the world in creative activity. Incompleteness of objects, multiplicity of systems of objects, are basic, ontological conditions of the possibility to act. The notion of action enables reference of a human being to the normative and natural order reproduced in concrete reality. It is through action that a subject introduces values into the natural world and gains self-awareness. Therefore, each activity is axionormative, that is, value-oriented. It is conducted with the aid of reflection and meanings,

---

227 Florian Znaniecki, *Wartości jako przedmioty kulturowe* (*Values as Cultural Objects*), in: Szacki, *Znaniecki*, p. 243.

as well as algorithms and rules that mediate in reaching objects (create norms). Action has a mediatising character, as it situates human beings and their references to values, meanings, cognition, finally to knowledge in the world of phenomena. Action mediates all relations of real world, at the same time being its part, it is real and creative, rational and experienced. Action also points to the subjective aspect of concrete reality, it is a category allowing to acknowledge the presence of consciousness in the real world. Action is objectifying, too, its results are new objects or new meanings of those already existing, as well as new values. A result of an action can be accessible to subsequent actions, experiences and reflection. Thus, as trans-actual, it acquires its objective existence. It is action that allows to include certain content of experience in different systems of objects. In consequence, states Znaniecki, it contains a "suggestion" of new relations between meanings. Therefore, a real object can undergo resubjectivisation by being given to consciousness actual in experience. The dynamics of action integrate the subjective part of concrete reality with the objective part, a subject with content, reflection with experience, duration with change. This way it becomes a connecting force for terms making up the intersubjective and trans-actual world of values and meanings.

* * *

Znaniecki and Ossowski realised that peculiarities or specificity of social sciences are actually a confirmation of ontological involvement of subjects taking part in social life. Thus a sociologist or another researcher of social life cannot neglect relations of this kind. As a matter of fact, both scholars' ideas concerning epistemological status of these sciences differ in intensity of ontological involvement. For Ossowski that involvement is a kind of necessary concession that an analytically unbiased researcher is compelled to accept in order to have any access to social world as the world of subjects coordinating their activities. So, we could risk a statement that Ossowski agrees to a philosophy that the tradition of the Lwów-Warsaw school did not accept, a philosophy where "life", including "social life", is an inextricable, although completely non-analytical, category. Therefore, through the back door, he introduces ideas officially undesired in the tradition of the Lwów-Warsaw school, but inevitable, it seems, on the ground of considerations on orders of life manifesting itself socially. Contrary to that, Znaniecki heads directly towards considerations whose purpose is to gain a possibly broad field of confrontation between metaphysical stances. The goal of this endeavour seems quite clear: on the ground of social research only such theories have a chance to succeed, which are ontologically involved, since only those can portray the entanglement of the research process produced by the humanistic coefficient. Znaniecki's ontology, the theory of concrete reality, that is also a theory of culture, compels to treat methodological aloofness (in the vein of Ossowski) as a result of scruples enforced by rather narrow metaphysics of the real world, dictated by naturalist prejudices. The history of sociology has rewarded Znaniecki, since in the second half of the 20th century sociology chose mainly a reflective and critical approach, conscious of its influence on social life and at the same time aware of influences it succumbs to (also in this sense it is a humanist discipline). Here sociology's criticism has a sense derivable from the tradition of Kant's philosophy, although the cognitive situation in the domain of sociology is not Kantian, as it concerns an object which is a subject (agent) entangled in relations with other subjects (agents). That is why reflectiveness of sociology also means that sociology cannot avoid the notion of subject in its reflective structure.

Conclusion

Social onto-epistemology (SOE) unequivocally embodies the ontological shift[228] which embraces even the traditionally anti-metaphysical analytic philosophy.[229] It shows possible ways of reaching beyond restrictions imposed by early modern philosophy's legacy. These restrictions involve epistemological fundamentalism, representationism, epistemocentrism, which are epistemological obstacles in the development of sociology, as well as other social sciences. Onto-epistemological venture beyond epistemology is stepping towards ways of conceptualising social life in categories of objectivity, rationality and intersubjectivity. This must entail such modifications of their meanings that would point at relations between ways of being and modalities of cognition and self-cognition. The modern and post-modern, or late modern form of common, social life environment, places them at the base of subjectivity. Therefore the one-sided cognitive reference of the subject to the object should be abandoned and the appropriate and a wide context of understanding and self-understanding should be employed, not overlooking the ontic situation of thinking, including theoretical thinking. It should not be overlooked that understanding takes part in interaction processes.

I think that not only relationality and dynamics are ontological properties of being, but also reflectivity, no longer construed epistemocentrically as the cognitive ability to capture something as an object, but involving

---

228 Cf. Andrzej Wojciech Nowak, *Wyobraźnia ontologiczna. Filozoficzna (re) konstrukcja fronetycznych nauk społecznych (Ontological Imagination. Philosophical (Re)construction of Phronetic Social Science)*, Instytut Badań Literackich PAN, Wydawnictwo Naukowe UAM, Poznań 2016; Bas van Heur, Loet Leydesdorff, Sally Wyatt, *Turning to Ontology in STS? Turning to STS Through 'Ontology'*, „Social Studies of Science" 2013, no. 43, June, pp. 341-362.

229 Cf. Charles B. Martin, John Heil, *Zwrot ontologiczny (The Ontological Shift)*, trans. M. Bucholc, T. Ciecierski, in: *Analityczna metafizyka umysłu. Najnowsze kontrowersje (Analytic Philosophy of Mind. The Latest Controversies)*, ed. Marcin Miłkowski, Robert Poczobut, Wydawnictwo IFiS PAN, Warszawa 2008, pp. 262-298.

the ontological extension of its meaning, as an ontic bond with the social environment. Thanks to self-awareness, reflectivity allows to understand the self and others. Reflectivity is the possibility to acquire social self-awareness at the level of a social actor and at the level of social theory. Reflectivity enables understanding not only as interpretation, but also as involvement. Our theoretical thinking is always situated somewhere, but this should not obscure the picture or obstruct developing social reflection, which science is, after all. Charles Taylor, writing about the objectives and the role of social sciences, stresses that in the effort to meet the requirements of the empiricist tradition, they reconstruct social reality in categories of raw data, hence one-sidedly. The price they pay is inability to grasp social reality in a way including intersubjective and common meanings as the characteristic trait of that reality. Taylor opines that our civilisation cannot be understood without investigating the process of communication aimed at agreement, i.e. without negotiations, which play a crucial role both in social practices and in theories justifying them.[230] It is hard not to agree with this diagnosis.

Such thinkers as e.g. Bourdieu, Giddens, Elias, as well as the earlier Znaniecki and indirectly also Ossowski, sociologists who were philosophers too, devised philosophies of social sciences that, investigating the ability and ways to gain knowledge of social reality, at the same time examine how conditions for this knowledge are shaped in this reality's manner of being, and how this knowledge participates in social reality. SOE fits into this strand of thinking, as it is a theory of social being concerning cognitive activities of subjects (social actors) and assuming participation of research achievements of these subjects in social reality. At the same time, it perceives ontic qualifications of social activities' participants as conditions of discoveries made. Asking about the possibility and ways of knowing social reality, we also ask how it exists and what provides the ontic base of its investigation. This cannot be separated without the loss caused by disregard of how knowledge and subjects are situated. That is why SOE is an attempt to step beyond transcendentalism, substantialism and essentialism

---

230 Cf. Charles Taylor, *Interpretation and the Sciences of Man*, "The Review of Metaphysics" 1971, vol. 25, no. 1, pp. 3-51.

in philosophy of social sciences (in philosophy of sociology) and, often tacit, presence of these approaches in these very sciences. Radical interpretational changes in the main traditions of 20th-century philosophy, affecting the philosophical discourse (e.g. rehabilitation of phenomenological tradition, neopragmatism, extra-philosophical influences of philosophical hermeneutics, philosophy of process etc.), were also reflected in social sciences.

Here it is worthwhile to consider where the departure from epistemocentrism in the area of social sciences has its sources. How does investigation of modern social phenomena support acceptance of the onto-epistemological approach? Helena Kozakiewicz, commentator of idea changes in the area of social thought, wrote:

> We need a new kind of epistemology, that could cope with the problem of inter-subjectivity. It requires a different form of rationality, not limited to discursivity; one able to understand 'quite practical practice', not fitting into 'categorical categories' and even the most 'critical' 'theory', to quote the unfashionable but not the least outdated, Marx.[231]

It must be added that, especially in sociology, we need a discourse examining the bonds among intersubjectivity, rationality and objectivity, as well as their dynamic and processual character. These bonds are revealed in the common social space, in the public sphere. Intersubjectivity guarantees a certain level of overtness of actions and thoughts, thus it allows to control their reference to the sphere of objects in social reality. It also gives cognitive access to other subjects, provided they take part in intersubjective orders regulating meanings of these actions and thoughts, hence in common interactional domains. This social objectivisation of actions in the form of practices is a prerequisite for the possibility to assess them, predicting their consequences and, above all, participation in them. Rationality and intersubjectivity function here as categories of social being. They can, exactly as categories of social being, be reflected (adequately or not) upon by social actors, they may also remain unarticulated, in the sphere of so-called tacit knowledge, a cultural competence, the skill of participating in a social process.

---

231 Kozakiewicz, *Epistemologia tradycyjna a problemy współczesności*, p. 180.

How are social actors' actions and thoughts, primarily objectivised in the public sphere, independent of mono-subjective consciousness, objectivised again by scientific investigation? Sociology has been stumbling upon this problem since its birth. The problem depends on the fact that between objectivisation performed by social actors and objectivisation executed by social researchers, the notions of rationality and intersubjectivity do not necessarily keep their meanings, yet they never lose their mutual links.

This issue has two essential aspects: sociological and epistemological. First, scholars creating secondary objectivisations of social being categories are also social actors, although they are equipped with diverse tools allowing to retain the stance of relative autonomy in relation to their objects. It is in scholars' communities, only relatively but in a way possible to capture sociologically, both standards of creating notions, their meanings, building theories out of them, and patterns of their application. They are created quite independently of ways they are formed, experienced, reflected upon in forms assuming participation of a social actor. That is why it is essential to examine forms of, in Bourdieu's terms, "objectivisation of the objectivising subject", reflexivity is important here. Second, it is impossible to "notionalise" categories of social being completely, because it is not possible completely to rationalise them and make them intersubjective, due to the inevitable (historical, cultural, maybe even biological) contingency of all thinking and investigation which chooses some form of people's being and life as an object.

Rationality poses an immanent problem in sociology. In SOE, social rationality, that is, both that referring to social life and that which is a topic in sociology, can be described as partial rationality. Nevertheless, we should take into account that it is a partial notion, i.e. not fully objectivised. Simultaneously, the way this notion is constructed prevents it from being universally intersubjective. This means that three categories of practical orders construed onto-epistemologically remain in certain interpretational dependences of one another. Rationality correlated with intersubjectivity is a requirement of human actions and thoughts, as long as these refer to other people's thoughts and actions possible to objectivise in some (scientific or not) order of knowledge. I see it in opposition to mono-subjective rationality, Cartesian style, or another monadic rationality, noting that one needs highly speculative verdicts concerning subjectivity and objectivity, i.e. these monads' harmony, in order to leave rationality's social character aside. Rationality and intersubjectivity, when they are impropriated and absorbed by substantial monads, do not leave any space between them. This state of affairs, or maybe state of thoughts, always requires a transcendent relation connecting them to be a coherent whole. When such a separation is performed, it also becomes necessary to leave aside history, tradition, language, culture. However, understanding, in hermeneutical take, as practising reason, is in advance, before determining its rationality and objectivity, intermediated by historicity, language, situated in a specific place, hence objectivised and rationalised in the contingent character of being human. This is where their crucial onto-epistemological bonds are manifest.

So, what is new about the theory of social reality proposed by SOE?

SOE shows that in the area of sociology basic notions have onto-epistemic character, they qualify not only epistemic properties of social actors, but also their ontic characteristics as subjects of cognition. In other words, sociology cannot be satisfied with recognising individual states of consciousness and summing them up. We cannot just summarise the existence of diverse stances with statistical calculations. Individual minds do not simply sum up because they are not sociological tokens; they communicate with one another, fight one another, co-operate with one another. During these acts of creating intersubjectivity they build themselves and change, again to return to interaction, already modified with their knowledge objectivising and rationalising their actions. The task of sociology, always reconstructive, should then follow the converse route: it should investigate processes in which different forms of intersubjectivity, through mutual influence, affect emergence of individual subjects with their knowledge, stances and regulated actions. Here relations are much more stable than objects they link, and cognition has the power of ontic causation, both in the subject and in the world.

"Onto-epistemology" is possibly a provisional term, transitional and imperfect, because it is drawn from vocabularies of traditions hereby criticised, but indicating reform of the basic conceptualisation of the cognitive relation in the area of social sciences. The modern epistemocentric zeal has directed the analysis of the cognitive relation so that nothing has remained between the subject and the object but the empty possibility of a relation. Though, it is sociology's matter to explore human *intermundia*. As a result, the dualism of opposing *res extensa* and *res cogitans* has become a trap for sociological thought. Therefore, within onto-epistemology the old notions of experience should be subverted and replaced with ones relying on intersubjectivity, which provides the essential area of seeking the meaning of experience, since it is intersubjectivity that fills the space between the subject and the world. Experience always refers to this, created and maintained together, space, the "between". Sociological analysis of intersubjectivity, contrary to approaches of classic epistemology, should be performed in a completely different way than suggested by epistemocentrism and representationalism: it should not reveal fixed universal characteristics of "representations", but living relations and ongoing processes: communication, co-operation and fight. These processes forge objects determined by their manners of social being, as well as subjects equipped with socially reproduced knowledge. To paraphrase Protagoras, it is the social being of humans that determines the measure of all things: existing ones, that they exist, and non-existent, that they do not. To paraphrase the equally old classic, Heraclitus, those who are vigilant and conscious, create the common world, intelligible for them; those asleep remain each in their own.

Defying the old Cartesian order, unfortunately we do not have too many other tools than those it has equipped us with for ages. It had established the modern way of thinking, involving mainly analysis: delving into details, atomising, dismantling the whole in order to examine. We rather look for simple than essential links, because we hope our discoveries will meet the requirement of knowledge universality. For the science about society it is not just an obstacle; it may even be a cognitive barrier.

However, respecting the obstinate confrontation between *res cogitans* and *res extensa*, we can reverse the direction of reasoning, beginning the deliberation from things already thought and as such inhabiting human worlds. Cognition, if it is not only an animalistic reaction to the environment, is always a social enterprise burdened with complex meanings and intellectual functions. Cognition would not make the least sense if its results could not be communicated. This makes cognition a social phenomenon at its very foundations. Not acknowledging it we could easily come to a radical conclusion, whose radicalism would not have been imaginable

for Descartes and his descendants: we would have to admit after one ancient classic that nothing exists. Human cognition is cognition with the
participation of an investigating Other, then it is also self-investigation.
Only in their background it is as well the sublime, scholastically detached,
as Pierre Bourdieu would have said, study of nature. Cognition is an ontic
dimension of human existence.

Bibliography

Amsterdamski Stefan, *Between History and Method: Disputes about the Rationality of Science*, trans. by Gene M. Moore, Olga Amsterdamska, Springer Science+Business Media, Dordrecht 2012.

Anderski Stanislav, *Max Weber's Insights and Errors*, Routledge, London 2010.

Arendt Hannah, *The Human Condition*, University of Chicago Press, Chicago 1998.

Aristotle, Aristotle in 23 Volumes, Vols. 17, 18, trans. by Hugh Tredennick, Cambridge, MA, Harvard University Press; London, William Heinemann Ltd. 1933, 1989.

Aristotle, *Posterior Analytics*, trans. by Jonathan Barnes, Oxford University Press, Oxford 1994.

Aristotle, *The Nicomachean Ethics*, trans. David Ross, Revised with Introduction and Notes by Lesley Brown, Oxford University Press, New York 2009.

Arystoteles (Aristotle), *Zachęta do filozofii (Protrepticus)*, trans. Kazimierz Leśniak, in: *Dzieła wszystkie (Collected Works)*, vol. 6, Wydawnictwo Naukowe PWN, Warszawa 2001, pp. 627–664.

Bachelard Gaston, *The Formation of the Scientific Mind. A Contribution to a Psychoanalysis of Objective Knowledge,* introduced, translated and annotated by Mary McAllester Jones, *Clinamen* Press, Manchester 2002.

Baert Patrick, Carreira da Silva Filipe, *Social Theory in the Twentieth Century and Beyond*, Polity Press, Cambridge 2010.

Bielińska-Hirszowicz Maria, *Reviewed Work:* O osobliwościach nauk społecznych [Special Characteristics of the Social Sciences] *by Stanisław Ossowski*, "The Polish Sociological Bulletin" 1963, no. 8, pp. 115–117.

Bińczyk Ewa, *Technonauka w społeczeństwie ryzyka. Filozofia wobec niepożądanych następstw praktycznego sukcesu nauki (Technoscience in Risk Society. Philosophy in the Face of Undesired Consequences of Science's Practical Success)*, Wydawnictwo Naukowe UMK, Toruń 2012.

Bourdieu Pierre and Wacquant Loïc J. D., *An Invitation to Reflexive Sociology*, Polity Press in association with Blackwell Publishers, The University of Chicago 1992.

Bourdieu Pierre, *Homo Academicus*, Les Éditions de Minuit, Paris 1984.

Bourdieu Pierre, *Le sens pratique*, Les Éditions de Minuit, Paris 1980.

Bourdieu Pierre, *Outline of a Theory of Practice*, trans. Richard Nice, University Press, Cambridge 1995.

Bourdieu Pierre, *Pascalian Meditations*, trans. Richard Nice, Stanford Univ. Press, California 2000.

Bourdieu Pierre, *Practical Reason: On the Theory of Action*, trans. Randal Johnson and others, Stanford University Press, California 1998.

Bourdieu. A Critical Reader, ed. Richard Shusterman, Wiley-Blackwell, Oxford 1999.

Bronk Andrzej, Majdański Stanisław, *Kłopoty z przyporządkowaniem nauk: perspektywa naukoznawcza (The Dilemma with Cognitive Categorization of Scientific Disciplines. A Methodological Point of View)*, „Nauka" 2009, no. 1, pp. 47–66.

Bytniewski Paweł, *Filozofia nauk, czyli epistemologiczne pożytki z historii poznania naukowego (Philosophy of Sciences, that is, Epistemological Advantages of History of Scientific Cognition)*, Filozofia i Nauka. Studia filozoficzne i interdyscyplinarne" 2014, vol. 2, pp. 113–134.

Bytniewski Paweł, *Trzy modele nieciągłego procesu historii nauk - Bachelard, Canguilhem, Foucault (Three Models of the Discontinuous Process of the History of Sciences - Bachelard, Canguilhem, Foucault)*, „Filozofia i Nauka. Studia filozoficzne i interdyscyplinarne" 2015, vol. 3, pp. 241–263.

Castells Manuel, *Rise of the Network Society*, Wiley-Blackwell, Oxford 1996.

Chałubiński Mirosław, *Stanisław Ossowski (Stanislav Ossowski)*, Wiedza Powszechna, Warszawa 2007. Curtius Ernst Robert, *Literatura europejska i łacińskie średniowiecze, (European Literature and Latin Middle Ages)*, trans. Andrzej Borowski, Universitas, Kraków 1997, pp. 309–357.

Czarnocka Małgorzata, *Podmiot poznania a nauka (The Knowing Subject and Science)*, Monografie Fundacji na rzecz Nauki Polskiej, Wrocław 2003.

Czerwiński Marcin, *Kultura i jej badanie (Culture and its Study)*, Zakład Narodowy im. Ossolińskich, Wrocław 1985.

Daston Lorraine, Galison Peter, *Objectivity*, Zone Books, New York 2007.

Daston Lorraine, Luncbek Elizabeth, *Histories of Scientific Observation*, The University of Chicago Press, Chicago, London 2011.

Descartes René, *Principles of Philosophy*, translated with explanatory notes, by Valentine Rodger Miller and Reese P. Miller, Kluwer Academic Publishers Dordrecht, Boston, London 1992.

Detienne Marcel, *The Masters of Truth in Archaic Greece*, trans. Janet Lloyd, Zone Books, New York 1999.

Elias Norbert, *Involvement and Detachment*, University College Dublin Press, Dublin 2007.

Evans-Pritchard Edward Evan, *Witchcraft, Oracles and Magic Among the Azande*, Oxford University Press 1976.

Ferguson Harvie, *Phenomenological Sociology. Insight and Experience in Modern Society*, SAGE Publications, London, Thousand Oaks, New Delhi 2006.

Fleck Ludwik, *Genesis and Development of a Scientific Fact*, trans. Fred Bradley and Thaddeus J. Trenn, ed. Thaddeus J. Trenn and Robert K. Merton, University of Chicago Press, 1981.

Foucault Michel, *Power/Knowledge. Selected Interviews and Other Writings 1972-1977*, ed. By Collin Gordon, trans. Colin Gordon, Leo Marshall, John Mepham, Kate Soper, Pantheon Books, New York 1980.

Foucault Michel, *Subjectivity and Truth*, in: Foucault Michel, *The Politics of Truth*, ed. Sylvère Lotringer, trans. Lysa Hochroth & Catherine Porter, Semiotext(e), Los Angeles 2007, pp. 147–167.

Foucault Michel, *The Archaeology of Knowledge and the Discourse on the Language*, trans. Alan Mark Sheridan-Smith, Pantheon Books, New York 1972.

Foucault Michel, *The Order of Things: An Archaeology of the Human Sciences*, Routledge, London, New York 2002.

Freeth Tony et al., *Decoding the Antikythera Mechanism: Investigation of an Ancient Astronomical Calculator*, „Nature" 2006, vol. 444, Issue 7119, pp. 587–591.

Fuller Steve, *Social Epistemology*, Second edition, Indiana University Press, Bloomington and Indianapolis 2002.

Gadamer Hans-Georg, *Teoria, etyka, edukacja. Eseje wybrane (Theory, Ethics, Education. Selected Essays)*, ed. Paweł Dybel, Wydawnictwo Uniwersytetu Warszawskiego, Warszawa 2008.

Gadamer Hans-Georg, *The Enigma of Health: The Art of Healing in a Scientific Age*, trans. James Gaiger and Nicholas Walker, Polity Press, Oxford 1996.

Gadamer Hans-Georg, *Truth and Method*, second revised edition, trans. revised by Joel Weinsheimer and Donald G. Marshall, Continuum, London, New York 2006.

Gadamer Hans-Georg, *Truth in the Human Sciences*, in: Brice R. Wachterhauser (ed.), *Hermeneutics and Truth*, Northwestern University Press, 1994, pp. 25-32.

Giddens Anthony, *The Construction of Society. Outline of the Theory of Structuration*, University of California Press, Berkeley, Los Angeles 1984.

Grenfell Michael, *Pierre Bourdieu. Agent Provocateur*, Conntinuum, London, New York 2004.

Habermas Jürgen, *Pojęcie działania komunikacyjnego. [Uwagi wyjaśniające] (The Notion of Communicational Activity [Explanatory Notes])*, trans. Andrzej M. Kaniowski, „Kultura i Społeczeństwo" 1986, no. 3, pp. 21–44.

Habermas Jürgen, *The Philosophical Discourse of Modernity. Twelve Lectures*, trans. Frederick D. Lawrence, Blackwell Publishers, Oxford 1998.

Habermas Jürgen, *The Theory of Communicative Action*, vol. 1: *Reason and the Rationalization of Society*, trans. Thomas McCarthy, Beacon Press, Boston 1984.

Hans-Georg Gadamer on Education, Poetry, and History Applied Hermeneutics, ed. by Dieter Misgeld and Graeme Nicholson, trans. Lawrence Schmidt and Monica Reuss, State University of New York Press, Albany 1992.

Heidegger Martin, *Being and Time*, trans. Joan Stambaugh, State University of New York Press, Albany 1996.

Heur van Bas, Leydesdorff Loet, Wyatt Sally, *Turning to Ontology in STS? Turning to STS Through 'Ontology'*, „Social Studies of Science" 2013, no. 43, June, pp. 341–362.

Hudzik Jan P., *Prawda w naukach społecznych (Truth in Social Sciences)*, in: *Prawda (The Truth)*, ed. Damian Leszczyński, Wydawnictwo Uniwersytetu Wrocławskiego, Wrocław 2011, pp. 363–394.

Intersubiektywność (Intersubjectivity), ed. Piotr Makowski, Wydawnictwo Universitas, Kraków 2012.

Judycka Joanna, *Paralelizm strukturalny projektów nauki uniwersalnej Lulla i Kartezjusza (Structural Parallelism of Llull's and Descartes's Projects of Universal Science)*, „Filo-Sofija" 2013, no. 22, pp. 213–229.

Judycki Stanisław, *Intersubiektywność (Intersubjectivity)*, in: *Powszechna Encyklopedia Filozofii (General Encyclopaedia of Philosophy)*, vol. 4, Polskie Towarzystwo Tomasza z Akwinu, Lublin 2003, pp. 893–894.

Kaesler Dirk, *Max Weber. Eine Einführung in Leben, Werk und Wirkung (Maz Weber. A Guide to Life, Work and Influences*, Campus Verlag, Frankfurt-New York 2003.

Kalinowski Jerzy, *Teoria poznania praktycznego (Theory of Practical Knowledge)*, Towarzystwo Naukowe Katolickiego Uniwersytetu Lubelskiego, Lublin 1960.

Kaniowski Andrzej M., *Filozofia społeczna Jürgena Habermasa. W poszukiwaniu jedności teorii i praktyki, (Jürgen Habermas's Social Philosophy. In Search of Unity of Theory and Practice)*, Kolegium Otryckie, Warszawa ca 1990, pp. 354–382.

Kant Immanuel, *Anthropology from a Pragmatic Point of View*, trans. Robert B. Louden, Cambridge University Press, 2006.

Koselleck Reinhart, *Futures Past on the Semantics of Historical Time*, Columbia Univ. Press, New York 2004.

Kotarbiński Tadeusz, *Dzieła wszystkie, t. I: Elementy teorii poznania, logiki formalnej i metodologii (Collected Works, vol. I: Elements of Epistemology, Formal Logic and Methodology)*, Ossolineum Wydawnictwo PAN, Warszawa 1990.

Kozakiewicz Helena, *Epistemologia tradycyjna a problemy współczesności. Punkt widzenia socjologa (Traditional Epistemology and Problems of Contemporaneity. A Sociologist's Point of View)*, in: *Borderlands of*

Epistemology, ed. Józef Niżnik, Wydawnictwo IFiS PAN, Warszawa 1992, pp. 155–180.

Kozakiewicz Helena, *Przyczynek do krytyki rozumu socjologicznego (A Contribution to the Critique of Sociological Reason)*, in: *Racjonalność, nauka, społeczeństwo (Rationality, Science, Society)*, ed. Helena Kozakiewicz, Edmund Mokrzycki, Marek J. Siemek, PWN, Warszawa 1989, pp. 357–375.

Kozakiewicz Helena, *Racjonalność i intersubiektywność. Epistemologiczne wyzwanie dla socjologii i filozofii (Rationality and Intersubjectivity. Epistemological challenges for Sociology and Philosophy)*, in: *Racjonalność współczesności. Między filozofią a socjologią (Rationality of Contemporaneity. Between Philosophy and Sociology)*, ed. Helena Kozakiewicz, Edmund Mokrzycki, Marek J. Siemek, PWN, Warszawa 1992, pp. 106–120.

Kozakiewicz Helena, *Zwierciadło społecznego świata (The Mirror of the Social World)*, PWN, Warszawa 1991.

Kuderowicz Zbigniew, *Dwie tradycje i dwa modele racjonalności (Two Traditions and Two Models of Rationality)*, „Studia Filozoficzne" 1983, no. 5–6, pp. 254–259.

Kuszyk-Bytniewska, *Działanie wobec rzeczywistosci. Projekt onto-epistemologii społecznej (Taking Action towards Reality. Blueprints of a Social Onto-Epistemology)*, Wydawnictwo Uiwersytetu Marii Curie-Skłodowskiej, Lublin 2015.

Kuszyk-Bytniewska Mariola, *Czy racjonalność jest „miejscem wspólnym" doświadczenia religijnego i naukowego? (Is Rationality a Common Place of Religious and Scientific Experience?)*, „Przegląd Religioznawczy" 2010, no. 4 (238), pp. 43–56.

Kuszyk-Bytniewska Mariola, *Dylemat rozumu scholastycznego: racjonalne kontra socjologiczne rekonstrukcje rozwoju wiedzy (Dilemma of a Scholastic Reason: Rational versus Sociological Reconstructions of the Development Knowledge)*, „Annales UMCS", sectio I, Philosophia-Sociologia, 2010, vol. XXXV, no. 2, pp. 195–205.

Kuszyk-Bytniewska Mariola, *Epistemocentrism as an Epistemological Obstacle in the Social Sciences*, „Dialogue and Univesalism" 2012, vol. 22, Issue 4, pp. 17–34.

Kuszyk-Bytniewska Mariola, *Osobliwości nauk społecznych a związki między filozofią i socjologią. Florian Znaniecki a Stanisław Ossowski (Special Characteristics of the Social Sciences and Relationships between Philosophy and Sociology. Florian Znaniecki and Stanislaw Ossowski)*, in: *Koncepcje socjologiczne Stanisława Ossowskiego a teoretyczne i praktyczne zagadnienia współczesności (Stanisław Ossowski's Sociological Ideas versus Theoretical and Practical Issues of the Present Day)*, red. Mirosław Chałubiński, Janusz Goćkowski, Iwona Kaczmarek-Murzyniec, Anna Woźniak, Biblioteka „Colloquia Communia" (47), Wydawnictwo Adam Marszałek, Toruń 2004, pp. 173–187.

Kuszyk-Bytniewska Mariola, *Rationality as an Onto-epistemological Category*, in: *Етносоціологічний та епістемологічний дискурс у науковому просторі [Ethnosociological and epistemological discourse in scientific space]*, eds. Volodymyr Yevtukh, Ryszard Radzik, Ganna Kisla, Інститут соціології, психології та соціальних комунікацій Національного педагогічного університету імені М. П. Драгоманова, Kiev 2013, s. 246–257.

Kuszyk-Bytniewska Mariola, *Zaangażowanie a neutralność – o trudnościach stosowania pojęcia obiektywności w naukach społecznych. Onto-epistemologiczna recepcja socjologii N. Eliasa (Involvement and Detachment. How to Understand the Inter-Subjectivity of the Social World and the Objectivity of Social Sciences? The Onto-Epistemological Reception of N. Elias' Sociology)*, „Roczniki Historii Socjologii" 2013, vol. 3, pp. 61–81.

Kuszyk Mariola, *Floriana Znanieckiego koncepcja rzeczywistości konkretnej. Przyczynek do nie-Husserlowskiej teorii doświadczenia*, w: *Studia z polskiej myśli filozoficznej 1900-1939 (Florian Znaniecki's Concept of Concrete Reality. A Contribution to non-Husserlian Theory of Experience*, in: *Studies on Polish Philosophical Thought 1900-1939* (ed. Leszek Gawor), Wydawnictwo UMCS, Lublin 1997, pp. 39–46.

Kwiatkowski Tadeusz, *Poznanie naukowe u Arystotelesa. Niektóre poglądy teoretyczne (Scientific Study in Aristotle's Thought)*, PWN, Warszawa 1969.

Lenk Hans, *Filozofia pragmatycznego interpretacjonizmu. Filozofia między nauką a praktyką. (Philosophy of Pragmatic Interpretationism. Philosophy between Science and Practice)*, trans. Zbigniew Zwoliński, Oficyna Wydawnicza Naukowa, Warszawa 1995.

176 Bibliography

Lévi-Strauss Claude, *Introduction of the Work of Marcel Mauss*, trans. Felicity Baker, Routledge and Kegan Paul, London 1987.

Lévi-Strauss Claude, *Structural Anthropology* vol. II, trans. Monique Layton, Basic Books, Inc., Publishers, New York 1975.

Lima Manuel, *The Book of Trees: Visualizing Branches of Knowledge*, Princeton Architectural Press, New York 2014.

Lisak Andrzej, *Marek J. Siemek and His Interpretation of the Idea of Transcendentalism*, "Dialogue and Universalism" 2016, no. 26(2), pp. 205–216.

Markiewicz-Lagneau Janina, *Florian Znaniecki: Polish Sociologist or American Philosopher?* "International Sociology" 1988, vol. 3, no. 4, pp. 385–402.

Martin Charles B., Heil John, *Zwrot ontologiczny (The Ontological Shift)*, trans. M. Bucholc, T. Ciecierski, in: *Analityczna metafizyka umysłu. Najnowsze kontrowersje (Analytic Philosophy of Mind. The Latest Controversies)*, ed. Marcin Miłkowski, Robert Poczobut, Wydawnictwo IFiS PAN, Warszawa 2008, pp. 262–298.

Mc Guire James E., Tuchańska Barbara, *Science Unfettered: A Philosophical Study in Sociohistorical Ontology*, Ohio University Press, Athens 2000.

Mead Georg Herbert, *Mind, Self, and Society. From The Standpoint of a Social Behaviorist*, The University of Chicago Press, Chicago and London 1972.

Mensch James Richard, *Intersubjectivity and Transcendental Idealism*, State University of New York Press, Albany 1988.

Merton Robert K., *Social Theory and Social Structure*, The Free Press, New York 1968.

Mills Charles Wright, *The Sociological Imagination* (40th Anniversary ed.), Oxford University Press, Oxford 2000.

Nowak Andrzej Wojciech, *Wyobraźnia ontologiczna. Filozoficzna (re)konstrukcja fronetycznych nauk społecznych (Ontological Imagination. Philosophical (Re)construction of Phronetic Social Science)*, Instytut Badań Literackich PAN, Wydawnictwo Naukowe UAM, Poznań 2016.

Ossowski Stanisław, *O osobliwościach nauk społecznych (Special Characteristics of the Social Sciences)*, PWN, Warszawa 1967.

Pierre Bourdieu: Key Concepts, ed. Michael Grenfell, Acumen Publishing Limited, Durham 2010.

Pomian Krzysztof, *Trzy modele poznania (Three Models of Cognition)* in: *Obecność. Leszkowi Kołakowskiemu w 60 rocznicę urodzin (Presence. For Leszek Kołakowski on his 60th Birthday)*, „ANEKS", London 1987, pp. 97–98.

Popper Karl R., *The Logic of the Social Sciences*; idem, *The Open Society and its Enemies*: Volume 1: *The Spell of Plato*, Princeton University Press, Princeton, New Jersey 1971.

Rorty Richard, *Philosophy and the Mirror of Nature*, Princeton University Press, Princeton, New Jersey 1979, pp. 129–311.

Rorty Richard, *Zmierzch prawdy ostatecznej i narodziny kultury literackiej (The Decline of Redemptive Truth and the Rise of a Literary Culture)*, „Teksty Drugie: teoria literatury, krytyka, interpretacja" 2003, no. 6(84), pp. 113–130.

Russo Lucio, *The Forgotten Revolution. How Science Was Born in 300 BC and Why It Had to Be Reborn*, trans. Silvio Levy, Springer Verlag, Berlin, Heidelberg, New York 2004.

Schütz Alfred, *Collected Papers*, vol. I: *The Problem of Social Reality*, ed. Maurice Natanson, Nijhoff, The Hague 1962.

Schütz Alfred, *The Problem of Rationality in Social World*, „Economica" 1943, vol. 10, no. 38, pp. 130–149.

Siemek Marek J., *Hegel i filozofia (Hegel and Philosophy)*, Oficyna Naukowa, Warszawa 1988.

Siemek Marek J., *„Nauka" i „naukowość" jako ideologiczne kategorie filozofii („Science" and „Scientism" as Ideological Categories of Philosophy)*, „Studia Filozoficzne" 1983, no. 5–6, pp. 71–84.

Siemek Marek J., *Transcendentalizm jako stanowisko epistemologiczne (Transcendentalism as an Epistemological Stance)*, in: *Dziedzictwo Kanta. Materiały z sesji Kantowskiej (Kant's Legacy. Materials from the Kantian Session)*, ed. Jan Garewicz, PWN, Warszawa 1976, pp. 17–57.

Siemek Marek J., *Wykłady z filozofii nowoczesności (Lectures on the Philosophy of Modernity)*, Wydawnictwo Naukowe PWN, Warszawa 2012.

Siemianowski Andrzej, *Poznawcze i praktyczne funkcje nauk empirycznych (Cognitive and Practical Functions of Empirical Sciences)*, PWN, Warszawa 1976.

Skarga Barbara, *Trzy idee racjonalności* (*Three Ideas of Rationality*), „Studia Filozoficzne" 1983, no. 5–6, pp. 17–37.

Social Cognition. Key Readings, red. David Hamilton, Psychology Press, New York 2005.

Szacki Jerzy, *Historia myśli socjologicznej. Wydanie nowe*, (*History of Sociological Thought*), PWN, Warszawa 2002.

Szacki Jerzy, *Znaniecki*, Wiedza Powszechna, Warszawa 1986.

Szaniawski Klemens, *Racjonalność jako wartość* (*Rationality as a Value*), „Studia Filozoficzne" 1983, no. 5–6, pp. 7–15.

Szawarski Zbigniew, *Mądrość i sztuka leczenia (Wisdom and the Art of Healing)*, Wydawnictwo słowo/obraz terytoria, Gdańsk 2006.

Taylor Charles, *Interpretation and the Sciences of Man*, "The Review of Metaphysics" 1971, vol. 25, no. 1, pp. 3–51.

Taylor Charles, *Overcoming Epistemology*, in: Charles Taylor *Philosophical Arguments*, Harvard University Press, Cambridge, London 1995, pp. 1–19.

Taylor Charles, *Sources of the Self. The Making of the Modern Identity*, Harvard University Press, Cambridge, Massachusetts 1994.

The Blackwell Guide to Epistemology, ed. John Greco & Ernest Sosa, Blackwell Publishers 2007.

The Lvov-Warsaw School and Contemporary Philosophy, ed. Katarzyna Kijania-Placek, Jan Woleński, Springer Science & Business Media, Dordrecht 1998.

Thomson Patricia, *Field*, in: *Pierre Bourdieu key Concepts*, ed. Michael Grenfell, Acumen Publishing Limited, Durham 2010, pp. 67–81.

Tuchańska Barbara, *Dlaczego prawda? Prawda jako wartość w sztuce, nauce i codzienności (Why Truth? Truth as a Value in Art, Science, and Everyday Life)*, Wydawnictwo Poltext, Warszawa 2012.

Vernant Jean-Pierre, *The Origins of Greek Thought*, Cornell University Press 1982.

Vidal-Naquet Pierre, *The Black Hunter: Forms of Thought and Forms of Society in the Greek World*, Johns Hopkins University Press 1986.

Voegelin Eric, *Aristotle, Order and History*, vol. 3, *Plato and Aristotle*, The Collected Works of Eric Voegelin, vol. 16, ed. Dante Germino, University of Missouri Press, Columbia 2000, pp. 325–428.

Walczak Monika, *Racjonalność nauki. Problemy, koncepcje, argumenty* (*Rationality of Science. Problems, Concepts, Arguments*), Towarzystwo Naukowe KUL, Lublin 2006.

Wiley Norbert, *Znaniecki's Key Insight: The Merger of Pragmatism and Neo-Kantianism*, "Polish Sociological Review" 2007, vol. 158, Issue 2, pp. 133–143.

Williams Malcolm, May Tim, *Introduction to the Philosophy of Social Research*, Routledge, London and New York 2000.

Winch Peter, *Understanding a Primitive Society*, "American Philosophical Quarterly" 1964, no. 1, pp. 307–324.

Wittgenstein Ludwig, *Tractatus logico-philosophicus*, Routledge, London-New York 2002.

Zaner Richard M., *Solitude and Society: The Critical Foundations of Social Science*, G. Psathas (eds.) *Phenomenology and Sociology*, Wiley-Interscience New York 1973, pp. 25–46.

Znaniecki Florian, *Cultural Reality*, The University Chicago Press, Chicago, Illinois 1919.

Znaniecki Florian, *Cultural Sciences. Their Origin and Development*, University of Illinois Press, Urbana 1952.

Znaniecki Florian, *Social Relation and Social Roles. The Unfinished Systematic Sociology*, Chandler Publishing Company, San Francisco 1965.

Znaniecki Florian, *The Method of Sociology*, Rinehart & Company, Inc. New York 1934.

Znaniecki Florian, *Wstęp do socjologii (Introduction to Sociology)*, PWN, Warszawa 1988.

Subject Index

Onto-epistemology *passim* 7, 9,
11-14, 33, 35-37, 55, 58, 86-90,
92, 108, 131, 134, 148, 153,
161, 165, 166
Ontology 7, 9, 36, 81, 88, 92, 97,
131, 150, 152, 159, 161

Peculiarities of social sciences
143, 147
Phenomena 11, 57, 70, 74, 77, 85,
90, 95, 123, 128, 138, 143, 145-
147, 153-155, 158, 163
Phenomenology 127, 129
Philosophy of sociology 58, 163
Phronesis 17, 46, 54
Poiesis 10, 16-20, 22-25, 27, 28,
34, 43, 104
Practical 7-9, 15-22, 24, 25, 27-
29, 32-36, 39, 41, 43, 44, 47,
48, 49, 51, 52, 54, 60, 61, 63,
65-68, 70-74, 77, 82, 86, 98,
100-108, 114, 118-122, 124,
126, 127, 129, 131, 133-136,
139-142, 145, 147, 152, 154,
163, 164
Praxis 10, 16-20, 23-25, 28, 29,
34, 35, 37, 42, 44, 46, 50, 52-
54, 72. 73, 98, 99, 102, 107,
118, 134, 153, 156

Rationality 8, 10, 11, 24, 25,
38, 41, 44, 47, 53, 62, 72, 75,
77, 78, 85, 87-89, 92, 94-105,
107, 108, 113, 128-132, 161,
163-165
– Procedural rationality 98, 100
– Substantial rationality 95, 97, 98
Reality 8-11, 13-16, 21, 28, 33,
44, 45, 48, 52, 57-59, 61-73, 75,
77, 80, 82-84, 87, 89, 92, 94,
95, 97-99, 101, 102, 104, 105,
107, 108, 116, 118, 123-125,

133, 136, 143, 145-147, 149-
159, 162, 163, 165
– Cultural reality 123, 149, 150,
152, 154, 155
– Concrete reality 124, 151-154,
156-158, 159
– Social reality 8-11, 13-15, 33,
44, 48, 58, 59, 63-65, 67, 71,
72, 75, 77, 89, 94, 98, 101, 102,
133, 136, 145, 150, 151, 162,
163, 165
Reason 11, 13-16, 18, 19, 22, 23,
33, 37, 41, 44, 51, 56, 58, 64-
66, 72-75, 84, 91, 95-98, 102-
105, 108, 109, 113, 124, 128,
130, 147, 165, 166
– Practical reason 44, 72-74,
104, 108
– Scientific reason 113
– Scholastic reason 51, 105
Reflection 8, 9, 34, 46, 47, 55, 60,
67, 68, 87, 93, 126, 133, 137,
139, 152-154, 157, 158, 162
Reflectivity 37, 47, 48, 49, 138,
151, 161, 162
Representationism 11, 33, 72,
87, 161

Sciences 7-11, 13-16, 20, 27, 30,
33, 35-39,
– Ancient 26, 37
– Human 30, 44, 45, 48, 51, 52,
59, 83-85, 88
– Modern 10, 26, 37, 38, 42, 44,
52, 60, 61, 64, 87, 156
– Natural 8, 26, 27, 43, 44, 51-53,
55, 59, 63, 64, 68, 79, 82-85,
90, 91, 98, 101, 102, 110, 112,
117-119, 121, 145-147, 157
– Practical 35, 48, 98, 102
– Social 7-11, 13-15, 30, 33, 37,
39, 44, 45, 47-50, 52, 54-61,

Names Index

Comparative Studies on Education, Culture and Technology
Vergleichende Studien zur Bildung, Kultur und Technik

Edited by / Herausgegeben von
Tomasz Stępień

Vol. / Bd.   1   Tomasz Stępień / Annette Deschner / Mojca Kompara / Adriana Merta-Staszczak: Spatialisation of Education. Migrating Languages – Cultural Encounters – Technological Turn. 2013.

Vol. / Bd.   2   Anton Hilckman: Gesammelte Werke. Schriften zur philosophischen Pädagogik Teil 1. Bildung – Begeisterung – Freiheit. Bearbeitet, kommentiert und herausgegeben von Tomasz Stępień. 2014.

Vol. / Bd.   3   Anton Hilckman: Gesammelte Werke. Schriften zur philosophischen Pädagogik Teil 2. Christliche Philosophie. Bearbeitet, kommentiert und herausgegeben von Tomasz Stępień. 2014.

Vol. / Bd.   4   Ewa Bińczyk / Tomasz Stępień: Modeling Technoscience and Nanotechnology Assessment. Perspectives and Dilemmas. 2014.

Vol. / Bd.   5   Tomasz Stępień: Heuristics of Technosciences. Philosophical Framing in the Case of Nanotechnology. 2016.

Vol. / Bd.   6   Mojca Kompara / Tomasz Stępień: Spatialisation of Higher Education: Poland and Slovenia. 2017.

Vol. / Bd.   7   Anton Hilckman: Gesammelte Werke. Schriften zur politischen Pädagogik. Teil 1: Politische Theorie und Föderalismus. Bearbeitet, kommentiert und herausgegeben von Tomasz Stępień. 2019.

Studies on Culture, Technology and Education

Edited by Krzysztof Abriszewski

Vol. / Bd.   8   Krzysztof Abriszewski / Aleksandra Derra./. Andrzej W. Nowak: Polish Science and Technology Studies in the New Millennium. 2022.

Vol. / Bd.   9   Mariola Kuszyk-Bytniewska: A Social Onto-Epistemology. 2023.

www.peterlang.com

Ingram Content Group UK Ltd.
Milton Keynes UK
UKHW011316310523
422605UK00003B/18